UNSOLVED
MURDERS
in new zealand

UNSOLVED MURDERS
in new zealand

by tony williams

Hodder Moa Beckett

ISBN 1-86958-724-3

© 1999 – Original text by Tony Williams
The moral rights of the author have been asserted

© 1999 – Design and format by Hodder Moa Beckett Publishers Ltd.

Published in 1999 by Hodder Moa Beckett Publishers Ltd
[a member of the Hodder Headline Group],
4 Whetu Place, Mairangi Bay, Auckland, New Zealand

Designed and produced by Hodder Moa Beckett Publishers Ltd.

Printed by Griffin Press, Australia

All rights reserved. No part of this publication may be reproduced or
transmitted in any form or by any means, electronic or mechanical,
including photocopying, recording, or any information storage and
retrieval system, without permission in writing from the publisher.

Contents

Acknowledgements

The idea for this book started with Tom Brown, who is perhaps New Zealand's leading crime buff. He suggested a book on unsolved murders then, when Hodder Moa Beckett agreed, Tom kindly lent me several books from his extensive crime library with which to begin my research.

My intention was for the book to be about the most intriguing of the unsolved murders in New Zealand's history.

I then turned to my panel of experts: Tom Brown; Jock Anderson, currently with the "National Business Review", who for many years was a crime reporter with "Truth" and other publications; and Chief Inspector Sherwood Young, the official police historian at Police National Headquarters in Wellington.

Sherwood assisted me throughout the writing of the book with intelligent advice and guidance, which is much appreciated. Note that access to police files, was declined on the basis that there was confidential information in the files that was being withheld until such time as each of the murderers might be brought before a court.

Most of my research therefore had to be done from secondary sources. I am very grateful to Cynthia Shaw of the Newsmedia Library, who was very patient and helpful.

I would also like to thank the staff of Manukau Libraries, who always go out of their way to be of assistance.

My thanks also to my typist and office assistant, Teresa Harvey.

When the book was as complete as I could make it, I attempted to track down the officers who had worked on the cases to verify the facts. Some of them had retired from the police force and others were unable to be contacted for other reasons, but I would like to thank the following for their assistance:

Jo Galer, Media Liaison Officer, Otago Police; Maggie Leask, Media Liaison Officer, Canterbury Police; Detective Senior Sergeant Bruce Raffan, Hamilton CIB; Bruce Scott, Assistant Commissioner Auckland; Detective Superintendent Ted Lines (retired); Detective Senior Sergeant Jim McCully; Detective Senior Sergeant Peter Mitford-Burgess, Otahuhu CIB; Detective Senior Sergeant Dayle Candy, Otahuhu CIB; former Detective Inspector Phil Jones (now Inspector at Queenstown Police); Richard Middleton, Auckland CIB.

I should point out that any assistance from the police was in the form of advice and guidance only and no part of this book should be construed in any way as presenting an official police view. I have tried to tell these stories by laying out the facts as they can be ascertained. Where opinions do intrude, they are mine and mine alone.

Introduction

This book is about the murderers who got away. Sometimes our only contact with them is their horrific deed and whatever meagre clues they left behind. Murder is the act of dispossessing another human being of life. It is a grotesquely intimate act usually committed in a solitude which the murderer shares only with his victim. For the murderer, it grows ever lonelier as he seeks to cover up his crime and escape apprehension.

Some of the murderers listed here will be dead, some of them may be in prison, convicted of other crimes, but some of them are no doubt still alive, living their lives quietly, keeping to the shadows and the quiet corners knowing that they possess a secret which they can share with no one else.

The purpose of the investigative process is simply to bring that secret into full view. The best investigators are rational, open minded and relentless. They follow what the police term "lines of inquiry" but which are probably better thought of as the track of a crime, in the same way that a bloodhound follows a scent.

Most murder investigations start with a body. Once the decomposition process sets in, the clues start to fade. A body discovered a week or more after death can often mask the cause.

Of the 17 cases in this book (18 bodies in all) that remain

unsolved, three of the bodies were never found (technically the people "disappeared" though all are the subject of murder inquiries) and another six were discovered after decomposition was well advanced.

Next the investigator must examine the scene of the crime, if known, for forensic clues. The first question he will ask himself is, "Was the body killed where it was found?"

In murder investigations, it is often inanimate objects that do the talking. A knife stained with the blood of the victim and marked with the fingerprints of the murderer will be a central piece of evidence.

In many ways, forensic testing is more reliable than the testimony of witnesses. People have failings of memory and perception. The essential details are often seen and/or reported differently. Two witnesses may see the same car and one say it is new, while another says it is old. The police often have to wade their way through a morass of apparently conflicting evidence.

Some of it may be hoaxes. During any murder investigation, there is usually a flood of ideas submitted by people who claim to have psychic intuition or just hunches. Such people have occasionally been correct and helped to solve crimes in the past and the police are loath to disregard any such information, willing to follow any clue that might lead to the resolution of the case.

The investigative process starts as widely as possible, then, following lines of inquiry, tends to focus on specific suspects. Further investigation eliminates some until one suspect remains.

The file for an unsolved murder is never closed. Though in time the search team might be scaled down and all the officers eventually assigned to other inquiries, any new lead will immediately be investigated.

As far as the police are concerned, two of the cases in this book are closed. In one of them, the murderer died before coming to trial. The other is the notorious case of the murders of Harvey and Jeannette Crewe.

As I mentioned earlier, I chose those cases that have most caught public attention in New Zealand's brief history. Many of the victims mentioned in this book have become household names and whether we like it or not we are on first-name terms with young women such as Kirsa and Mona. In many ways, we have adopted them, or at least their memory, as we help to search for their murderers.

In many of the cases here, the police are certain who committed the murders but could not bring a conviction because of a lack of evidence. In some of the cases, the chief suspects have died soon afterwards, perhaps their demise accelerated by their guilt.

Compared to most other countries, New Zealand is underpopulated and the majority of the unsolved murders here have occurred in open spaces. Betty Marusich, for instance, was murdered in an open space in the middle of New Zealand's largest city.

Cars have also been an essential part of most of these murders, enabling the killers to get away quickly from the scene.

One strange fact is of the total of 17 victims listed here, nine of them were either on holiday or about to go on holiday. Why should this be? I believe that it is because in a holiday frame of mind people relax and are less alert to what is going on around them.

Each of the situations in this book is different. Several of the murder victims in these pages skirted too close to the periphery of the law and suffered the consequences. Others, it seems, had secluded lives that did not prepare them for evil when it suddenly appeared. They simply were not ready and paid the ultimate penalty.

NOTE

Old murders do get solved. For that reason, the names of witnesses are generally not used here, as they may be called on in the future to give evidence in a court of law.

Unsolved Murders
1902-1999

This is a list of unsolved murders but there may be others not on this list. Some of them are technically "disappearances" rather than murders, though in these cases it can be strongly suspected that murder is the reason why the missing person was never seen or heard from again.

Also, by my definition, "unsolved" means that no one was ever convicted of the murders in a court of law (or would have been if they had not died or been killed in the process of being arrested). In the case of Nina Chibba, for example, who disappeared from Hawera in 1931, a man was charged, but acquitted.

Nor does it include cases where the likely identity of the murderer was known to the police but that person was found not guilty by reason of insanity. There will also be cases currently pending where persons stand accused of outstanding murder cases. None of these is included in this list.

1902   • Unknown woman's body found in harbour, Wellington

1914   • 8 September, Francis Marshall, Auckland

1916
- January, Horatio Ramsden, Auckland
- 11 May, Mr and Mrs Holland, Kaiapoi

1921
- 17 July, Francis Jew, 20, Auckland
- 26 August, James Dorgan, Timaru

1923
- 26 October, Margaret Oates, 32, Wanganui

1927
- 5 November, Allen Cornell, Hamilton

1928
- October, Elsie Walker, 16, Auckland

1931
- Nina Chibba, 5, Hawera
- October, Arthur Blomfield

1933
- 18 November, Donald Fraser, Christchurch
- October, James Hunter Blair, Mt Roskill, Auckland

1935
- 2 July, Joan Rattray, 6, Napier

1936
- 3 June, Ernest Severin Nelson, Waihou Valley

1942
- 8 August, Annie and Rosamund Smyth, 62 & 72, Wairoa

1945
- 12 May, Edward Clarke, 22, Hamilton

1946
- 4 February, Herbert Miles Radcliffe, 52, Wellington

1947
- 7 July, Marie West, 17, Wellington
- 21 April, Francis Wilkins

1948
- 17 December, Herbert Brunton, 69, Wairoa

1949
- 28 September, William McIntosh, 63, Central Otago
- 1 October, Gordon Pepper, 24, Auckland

1961
- Wendy Mayes, Wellington

1962
- 6 February, James Ward, Dunedin

1970
- 31 December, Jennifer Beard, 25, West Coast
- 15 May, Olive Walker, 18, Rotorua
- 17 June, Harvey and Jeannette Crewe, Pukekawa

1975
- 31 May, Mona Blades, 18, Napier

1976
- 29 January, Tracey Ann Patient, 13, Auckland

1979
- 5 July, George Englebrecht, 94, Wellington

1980
- 16 August, Alicia O'Reilly, 6, Auckland

1982
- 3 June, Alfred Anderson, Christchurch

1983
- May, Adrian Smith, Gisborne
- 1 September, Kirsa Jensen, 14, Napier

1984
- 27 March, Ernie Abbot, 63, Wellington

1985
- 15 December, Brent Minhinnick, 23, Hamilton

1986
- 5 June, Luana Deborah La Verne Williams, Tauranga

1987
- 19 July, Teresa Cormack, 6, Napier
- 24 October, Chris Bush, 43, Maramarua
- 26 December, Maureen McKinnel, 38, Queenstown

1988
- 31 May, Martin Reid, 27, Rangiora
- 9 November, Joanne Chatfield, Auckland

1989
- 8 September, Garth Doull, 42, Wellington

1992
- 17 October, Amber-Lee Cruickshank, Kingston
- 28 October, Judith Yorke, 25, Te Puke

1993
- 5 May, Kevin O'Loughlin, 30, Nelson
- 26 May, Jane Furlong, Auckland

1994
- 7 February, Norrie Triggs, 51, Wellington

1995
- 26 January, Stuart Te Wano, 21, Ruatoria
- 17 August, Angela Blackmore, Christchurch
- 19-21 September, Betty Marusich, Auckland

1996
- 26 July, Tania Furlan, Auckland

1997
- 24 September, Nancy Frey-Herschey, Great Barrier Island

1998
- 28 April, Claire Elizabeth Hills, Auckland
- Lien Nguyen, Auckland
- 11-14 September, Kayo Matsuzawa, Auckland

1. Elsie Walker

A Killer with a
Shrewd and
Practical Mind

On 5 October 1928, the body of a young woman was discovered lying near Mt Wellington, in south Auckland. At about 8.15 pm that evening, a young man had been hurrying along an area of wasteland beside the mountain when he stumbled over it lying right in his path. The shocked youth quickly hurried home and phoned the police.

Constable Graham, the policeman whom the young man led to the body, filed the following report: "The body was lying with the feet and part of the legs protruding from the bushes. There was no disarrangement of clothing. Rodents had gnawed at exposed arms and throat. Congealed brown fluid had come from the mouth to the neck. It could have been a poisonous substance. I examined the clothing for identification. There was none. I could not determine the cause of death. There was no sign of a struggle. The face was distorted and I could not make a reasonable guess at the female's age."

The coat the woman was wearing was pulled up over the back of her head as if someone had gripped it there to drag her body through the scrub to its final resting place.

At first, it was not clear how she had got there or what had been the cause of death. Apart from the "distorted expression" on her face, there were no other signs of distress or marks or injuries on her body. Her clothing had not been interfered with. There was nothing that indicated she had suffered a violent death. Perhaps she had been out at night, had wandered to this lonely spot and lain down and died of exhaustion or of cold.

Her identity was soon discovered to be that of 16-year-old Elsie Walker. Elsie was slim and of average height with thick, dark hair and brown eyes. She was a country girl who had been born on a farm near the small settlement of Raukokore on the East Coast. She had a normal country life, with five younger children to look after. But it seemed she yearned for something more.

She had a pen-friend in Auckland who wrote her letters full of her life in Auckland. To young Elsie, the social life there sounded very exciting with parties and new people to meet. The two formulated a plan that Elsie would come to Auckland and get a job. They would share a flat and do the social rounds together.

However, Elsie's parents were horrified by this idea. They obviously thought that their impressionable young daughter being let loose in the wicked big city was too terrible to contemplate. They reached a solution where Elsie would go and stay with her uncle Frank Bayly who owned a large farm at Papamoa, near Tauranga.

There Elsie would be safe in the family environment and just one mile away was the town of Te Puke, where there were many social activities the eager young girl could engage in.

By a bizarre coincidence, there was to be a notorious disappearance from a dance at Te Puke more than 60 years later. In 1990, at the age of 23, attractive Judy Yorke visited a palm reader who warned her that she would die young. It was a prediction she took very seriously. She often told friends and relatives that they would miss her when she was gone. They just laughed about it.

Then on 21 October 1992, she went to a dance in an orchard packing shed near Te Puke. She was never seen or heard of again. Her body has never been discovered.

Also in the month of October, this time on the 1st, in 1928, Elsie Walker told her uncle and aunt that she was going to a dance.

She had been living on her uncle's farm for a year before her death. She was a useful addition to the family as her uncle and aunt had four sons and no daughters. Two of the sons lived at home and two had moved away. Elsie was allowed complete freedom to come and go within the household, but even then, did she have a yearning for even greater excitement?

She was last seen in the kitchen of the farmhouse at about 8 pm on the evening of 1 October. She was dressed in her "kitchen clothes" because she had just helped her cousin to do the dishes. She never went outside in her kitchen clothes and only ever wore them around the house. Yet these were the clothes she was wearing when her body was found on the wasteland in Mt Wellington.

At about 2.30 am on the morning of 2 October, the elder of the two Bayly boys, who was living at the farm, returned home from his social activities and noticed that one of the family cars, a Whippet, was not in its usual place in the garage. He thought nothing of it and went to bed.

The father, Frank Bayly, rose early and at about 6 am he was passing the garage when he also noticed the Whippet was missing. He returned to the house to find out who had taken it and in the course of his investigation it was discovered for the first time that Elsie had not returned the previous evening. He immediately contacted the police.

The car was discovered on 3 October abandoned at Papatoetoe, Auckland, about 15 miles from where her body was discovered. Frank Bayly stated there had been enough petrol in the car's tank to drive the 180 miles from Papamoa to Auckland. Police dusted the car for fingerprints but none was found.

How did Elsie and the car get to Auckland? And why were her body and the car discovered so far apart?

It was uncertain if Elsie knew how to drive a car. There was some talk that she had been seen learning to drive on the farm driveway. One theory was that she had taken the car herself and driven to Auckland alone. Why she might have done such a thing was unclear. She was on good terms with her aunt and uncle and despite her hankering to see the big city, there did not seem to be any good reason why she should "steal" the family car and run away to Auckland.

It also seemed very unlikely that an inexperienced driver could have navigated those country roads in the dark. Additionally, a punctured tyre was found in the boot of the car. Could a slender, inexperienced girl have changed it or would she have had to call into a garage to get it done?

Then did she abandon the car in Papatoetoe for some reason and start walking towards Auckland?

After Elsie's photo appeared in the newspaper, a delivery boy for the "New Zealand Herald" came forward to say he had seen Elsie walking from Auckland to Papatoetoe on the morning of 2 October at about 6 am.

On that same morning, a milkman said that he saw Elsie walking along Panmure Rd. The time of the milkman's sighting was 5.30 am, which would seem to contradict the earlier sighting. His was given more credence as his description of the clothes she was wearing was more accurate.

The other alternative is that she was driven to her death by someone she knew.

Inquiries were made along the route from Auckland to Papamoa, at garages and stores, to try to discover if anyone had sighted the person who might have driven her along those twisting country roads on that dark night or assisted to change the punctured tyre, but no leads as to the potential identity of the driver were found.

The post mortem revealed that she had been dead for several days. It was likely that she had died either on the evening of 1 October or the early hours of the morning of 2 October. The pathologists discovered a small bruise under Elsie's scalp, which was not visible from the outside. It was about the size of a small coin.

Again this new piece of evidence posed more questions than it solved. If she had driven herself to Auckland, could it have resulted from her head striking against the bodywork of the car after the wheel struck a pothole on the rough country roads?

Medical evidence was later to rule out this possibility. It was believed that the blow would have caused immediate unconsciousness, so that she could not have driven herself to Auckland and staggered to the spot where she died.

At first, the pathologists had believed that Elsie had died of exhaustion or natural causes, but two months later they reviewed their findings. By that time, Elsie had been dead for two months and though they did not exhume the body, their second set of findings was now radically different from the first.

They now stated, "The probable cause of death was concussion, following a blow on the head." This dramatic change of view was probably explained by the fact that, though the two men were experienced doctors, they were not experienced in pathology.

If the bruise had been caused by another party, had it been intentional or simply an act of carelessness? Was this a case of murder or accidental death and if it was the latter, why hadn't the person who had been with Elsie that night come forward?

An inquest was held five months after Elsie's death. During it, the newspapers described one man as "the mystery witness". He was William Bayly, the 25-year-old son of Mr and Mrs Frank Bayly, who was also Elsie's cousin. Bayly was a handsome man with darkly intelligent, almost cunning eyes. He was also known to be something of a ladies' man.

He had visited the family farm often, apparently got on well with Elsie and had often escorted her to dances before his own marriage to Phyllis on 29 August 1928. But Elsie had made no secret of her attraction to her older and very dashing cousin.

Bayly lived with his wife on his own farm, which was just ten miles away from his father's farm, but on the night that Elsie disappeared he claimed to have been living in a boarding house in Auckland.

Rumours began to fly around that William Bayly and Elsie had been lovers. At the inquest, evidence was given which seemed to refute this. A letter was produced written by Elsie in which she pleasantly referred to William Bayly's engagement to his future wife.

Bayly testified at the inquest that on 1 October he had been at home in his boarding house in Auckland at about 11 pm. This was confirmed by witnesses. Despite this, many continued to harbour suspicions against William Bayly.

At the end of the inquest, the coroner found that, "Elsie Walker died about 1 October, somewhere between Papamoa and Auckland, and that the cause of death was concussion following a blow to the head, but whether that blow was accidental or homicidal, there was no evidence to determine."

Given the evidence, this was a proper verdict for the

coroner to make but neither the public nor the newspapers were satisfied. There is no doubt that many viewed Bayly as the guilty party. There is a curious photograph of him leaving the courthouse one day during the hearing. A middle-aged woman companion is looking across at him with a half-smile, an emotion akin to relief on her face. But Bayly's head is down, his eyes looking at something he is doing with his hands. He seems preoccupied by something else far away in time and place.

One weekly newspaper ran stories that were very critical of the police, suggesting that they had allowed a murderer to remain free. They illustrated these articles with photographs of Elsie Walker, the Bayly family and the car that had been driven that fateful night.

The result was a sudden overwhelming surge of evidence from the public, much of it of a rather dubious nature. One man came forward who claimed to have seen the car driven by a man on the road to Auckland that night. He even remembered the numberplate of the car, which was exactly the same as the Bayly car. Though the incident had occurred almost a year earlier, the car number was still fresh in the man's memory. He claimed to have made a conscious effort to memorise it when he had seen it, yet he could give no reason for this very unusual action.

It was a full eight months after the death of Elsie that two neighbours of the Baylys came forward. These sisters stated on the night of 1 October they had witnessed William Bayly on a train from Auckland to Te Puke. If that were the case, Bayly would have been able to have driven Elsie back to Auckland. But when their evidence was reviewed by T.M. Wilford, the Minister of Justice (he later became Sir Thomas Wilford, High Commissioner for New Zealand in London), in a statement to the House of Representatives, said that he considered their evidence to be entirely untrustworthy. (There was also a suggestion that one of the women had tried to blackmail Bayly's mother.)

Over 15,000 people signed a petition for Wilford to reopen the inquest, but after reviewing the new evidence, he found little of merit and categorically stated that he refused to assist in what "could only be a farce".

A commission of inquiry had been held into the investigation in June 1929 and chaired by Mr E. Page. His findings were that the police inquiries had been thorough and proper.

But those investigations had come to a grinding halt. It didn't stop tongues wagging in the Tauranga district and Bayly left the area and took his family to a farm at Ruawaro, seven miles northwest of Huntly. From the road, the farm sloped steeply back towards the marshes of Lake Whangape. There, the immediate neighbours were a farming couple, Samuel Pender Lakey and Christobel Lakey.

Samuel Lakey had emigrated to New Zealand from England in 1913. Ironically, he had soon been shipped back overseas to fight in the First World War. He survived the hell of Gallipoli, where he was wounded, to be discharged from the Army in 1918. This time when he came back to New Zealand, he brought with him his Welsh wife Christobel.

On his return, he purchased the small cottage and farm at Ruawaro, where William Bayly would become his neighbour many years later. The marriage produced no children, but Christobel Lakey made up for this to some degree by an affection for animals. She had a particular affinity for ducks and had a special concrete pond built for them in the corner of the garden part of their property.

Bayly was a very capable farmer but it seemed he always attracted trouble in his relations with others. He began to get into conflicts with his neighbours, particularly Samuel Lakey, with whom he had a dispute over some sheep. There was also an accusation from Bayly that on one occasion Lakey had borrowed his bull to service his own cows.

A statement given by Phyllis Bayly later said that she

had not been to the Lakey household for two years because, "my husband did not get on well with the Lakeys".

On one occasion, Bayly had threatened to shoot Lakey. Lakey took the threat seriously. He had to. Only a fence and a patch of ground divided them. All Bayly had to do one night was to cross the fence, creep through the darkness and he could easily shoot Lakey dead. Because of the slope of the land, there would be no chance of seeing him from the road above.

During an argument with Bayly a few days before he died, Lakey let slip some careless words. He said, "Your guilty conscience is pricking you. You murdered Elsie Walker and we expect the same."

On Monday 16 October 1933, a neighbouring farmer, Rod Cowley, noticed the Lakeys' cattle were still in the night pens and to his experienced eye were obviously unmilked. He called on another neighbour, John William Slater, and the two men went to investigate.

They knocked on the door but there was no answer. The Lakeys were not to be found outside the property or in the cowshed. Inside the house, they were shocked to find a carefully prepared evening meal uneaten. Immediately, they phoned the police and, being practical farmers, they milked the cows while waiting for them.

Then one of the men noticed a gumboot sticking out from underneath a pile of sacks by the pond. When the sacks were removed, they found the dead body of Christobel Lakey lying face down in the water. At first they thought she must have suffered a seizure, but this did not explain why her body had been obscured by sacks nor did it explain the bruising on her face. Her right eye had almost been completely dislodged from its socket.

Samuel Lakey was nowhere to be found. A suit of his clothes and a pair of gumboots were missing along with a shotgun and .22 rifle. It seemed that after arguing with his wife and murdering her, he disappeared into the countryside either intending to evade capture or to kill himself.

On 9 November, a reward of £100 was posted for "the discovery of or information leading to the discovery of Samuel Pender Lakey, if alive, or of his body, if dead".

An extensive search was made for Lakey. Men scoured the countryside and the burning slagheap of a coal mine was raked over to try to find him. After three days with no sign of him, it was decided he had either left the district entirely or was closer to home.

A meticulous search was made of the Lakey property. Again, the local knowledge of the close-knit farming community came to bear on the situation. On the property was an old, wheeled frame, which, as often happens on farms, had stood unused for years beside the woolshed. It was now found in a paddock next to the boundary fence. When the searchers inspected it, they found bloodstains which someone had apparently tried to hide by whittling away the wood. The fence formed the boundary to Bayly's property.

On the other side, they saw marks of the runners of a sledge in the grass. It was almost as if something had been brought to the fence on the wheeled frame, then transferred onto the sledge and taken away. When the sledge was examined by the police, they found a small bloodstain on the front board.

The evidence against Bayly quickly began to mount. Another bloodstain was found on a pair of dungaree trousers owned by Bayly. Bayly was unable to account for 200 rounds of ammunition which he had bought with a .22 Spandau pea rifle three days before the disappearance of the Lakeys. He claimed it must have been stolen.

But there was still not enough evidence to charge Bayly. The next breakthrough came from officers investigating a separate complaint about a neighbour's dog. Scrapings were taken from a long-handled shovel. When they were analysed, they were found to contain charcoal, wood and burnt sack and bone. On 30 October, the missing Lakey rifles were dug up out of the swamp at the bottom of Bayly's property.

Bayly claimed the rifles must have been "planted" there in an effort to frame him, but after a report that a pall of smoke had hung over his cowshed on the evening the Lakeys had disappeared, the police took away a half-drum from his 44-gallon drum for analysis.

William Bayly must have known what they would find and probably felt the noose beginning to tighten around his neck. He decided to get away. The police suspected he might try to escape and posted a guard. There are two accounts of how Bayly got away. One was that he rode a horse, hiding behind it Indian-style past the police sentinels. The other is that he donned an old pair of trousers and walked seven miles through the swamps to the roadside where friends were waiting to pick him up.

He left a note to his wife which read:

"My darling Philly,
Yesterday in Auckland I received definite
information that the police were going to try and
put the blame of Mrs Lakey's death and Lakey's
disappearance onto me. They have to vindicate
themselves somehow after the blunders they have
been making in the search for Lakey, and think
that I will be the easiest one to catch. As you
know, I was with you that night, but do not intend
to let them put their dirty tricks on me. I have
picked out a nice spot to rest in, so love to you and
the kids dear."

While they tracked him down, the police kept digging at Bayly's farm and kept finding more gruesome exhibits that finally numbered 251 at his trial.

They included pieces of burnt bone, burnt pieces of clothing, the charred heel of a boot, burnt buckles and buttons and the metal fittings from braces. In the sheep dip, they found Lakey's cigarette lighter, a part of his skull, a lock of his ginger hair and shotgun cartridges that had been mutilated to try to disguise their exit markings.

They found Lakey's watch scattered in small pieces around Bayly's property. The back of it had been cut in two to try to disguise identification then the two pieces thrown away far apart from each other.

In the orchard among grass which grew several feet high, the searchers found the petrous bone from one of Lakey's ears, part of the joint of his elbow and two pieces of his upper dentures.

Finally on 4 December, Bayly was arrested at a house in Green Lane, in Auckland. Six days later, he was charged with the murder of Samuel Lakey.

He came to trial before Mr Justice Herdman in the Auckland Supreme Court in May 1934, charged with the murders of both Samuel and Christobel Lakey.

Before the trial proper began, Justice Herdman gave the jury the following admonition, "I understand that, some years ago, the accused was linked with the death of a young woman. At no time was it proven, or indeed seriously suggested, that the accused who now stands in the dock, charged with multiple murder, was in any way connected with that matter. You must dismiss from your minds anything you have heard or read of this affair."

The prosecution was led by Vincent (later Sir Vincent) Meredith who had had previous dealings with Bayly, having represented the Crown interest at Elsie Walker's inquest.

At the time, the trial was the longest in New Zealand's criminal history. It lasted for five weeks and produced 483 pages of typed transcript of evidence given by 68 witnesses.

The jury took 70 minutes to come to the decision that Bayly was guilty. There was very strong circumstantial evidence against him and he had no alibi. According to the testimony of his wife, on the night of the murders, he had gone to milk the cows at about 5 pm and returned at about 7.45 pm.

At some time between about 8 to 8.30 am on the following day, 16 October, Bayly was seen by a neighbour, Mrs Stevens, riding a horse onto the Lakey property. Shortly afterwards, she saw him riding a sledge that was being pulled by his horse.

Perhaps the most damning evidence against him of all, though, was the silent testimony of the dead Christobel Lakey. When investigating the murder, the police found an envelope in the Lakey house. It was dated 9 January 1933 and addressed to Mr Frank Bayly, William Bayly's father. Tragically, it had never been sent.

Inside it said:

"Dear Mr Bayly,
I am writing to ask you if you could make it
convenient to come and see us. I am so sorry to
trouble you but Bill is on the warpath again with
his spiteful annoyances. We don't want to send for
the police until we have given you a chance to
settle with him. He will have to be made to keep
the peace. We are sick of his dirty spite. Please
come and we will tell you all. We have waited for
the Christmas holidays to go before writing and I
hope that the New Year will be a happier one for
you and Mrs Bayly and the family.
Believe me,
Yours faithfully,
Christobel Lakey."

Why didn't Christobel Lakey send the letter she had obviously written in such desperation? If she had done so, it might have saved her life.

William Bayly was sentenced to death and hanged in July 1934. Apparently he did not die straightaway. He had told the hangman, "Not too tight," when the noose was being put around his neck. As he hung from the gallows, an officer had to cling onto his legs to help end his life. He was probably unconscious at the time but it took four minutes before his pulse finally ceased to beat.

The Bayly case is intriguing from the point of view of the question, "What happens to a man who gets away with murder?"

Bayly's chief defence counsel at his trial was the eminent Erima Northcroft (later to be knighted). Junior counsel was Leonard Leary (later to become a QC). In his autobiography, "Not Entirely Legal", Leary describes Bayly as a courageous man.

He said that the day before he died, Bayly wrote a letter to his defence counsel which read:

"To Mr Northcroft and Mr Leary,
Dear Sirs,
I would like you both to know that I realise you
both did your very best for me during the trial. No
man can do more, and I would not like either of
you to think that I in any way think that your
counsel was not at all times in my best interests
& I do not think that you are in any way to blame
for the outcome.
The deck was stacked against me and coupled
with the past you made the most of heavy odds
and all I can do now is thank you for your best
endeavours on my behalf.
Yours faithfully,
W A Bayly."

In his book, Leary appears to take the point of view that Bayly could have been innocent of murder, but guilty of an unfortunate and accidental double manslaughter to which Lakey contributed by attempting to shoot him. There may be an element of truth in this. The two men appeared to be primed for a feud. This might explain why one of Bayly's cartridge cases was found on Lakey's property and why one of Lakey's was found on Bayly's property – though there might be other reasons for this too.

There was no real evidence to link Bayly with the murder of Elsie Walker. Yet what state of mind would it create for a man that everybody did believe he had committed a brutal murder? Knowing this, could someone, another neighbour, who had a grudge against both Lakey and Bayly, settle the matter by killing Lakey and framing Bayly? Possible but unlikely.

In Sherwood Young's book "Guilty on the Gallows", he records the account of the Reverend George Moreton, who attended to Bayly in his last days. "...He was, my whole instinct told me, a killer with an inexplicable contempt for personal danger; his mind was shrewd and practical and rather humourless – all qualities that have made great generals as well as great murderers; but he lacked breadth and vision – deficiencies that reduced his character to the commonplace. I talked to him; I listened to him for many hours in the weeks before he died on the gallows, but never once could I doubt that he was the murderer of Samuel and Christobel Lakey..."

It seems certain that Bayly killed the Lakeys. The circumstantial evidence was just too damning. Only Bayly would have used his own 44-gallon drum. Only Bayly would have had the time and opportunity to attempt to scatter Lakey's watch so widely over his property.

If Bayly did commit the murders of the Lakeys, it allows us a door into his mind. Is the following what happened that day?

Three days before the deaths, Bayly bought a Spandau rifle.

He knew the Lakeys were creatures of habit. Mrs Lakey would put the evening meal on, then they would milk the cows. Once they had finished, they would go back to the farmhouse and eat the evening meal.

They were seen from the road by a neighbour as they made their way down to the milking shed at about 4.30 pm that Sunday evening. Bayly saw them too. His rifle clutched in his hands, he made his way stealthily over towards the Lakey property, out of sight of the road. For the last few days, he had been going off to shoot pests, thus establishing a normal pattern of behaviour to his wife at that time.

Christobel Lakey came out of the shed first. She left her husband to finish the last of the milking while she walked up to the house to put the food on the table. He would sit straight down to a hot meal.

But then suddenly she found Bayly standing in front of her. Before she could cry out, he struck her with the butt of the rifle. She stood and tried to defend herself, but he struck again and again until she fell to the ground.

Barely conscious, he dragged her over to the pond and held her head down. At first she struggled and he saw bubbles rising in the water, but then the movements and the bubbles ceased. He held her there a little longer in case she was trying to deceive him. All the time, he kept his eye out for Samuel Lakey.

One reason he did not shoot Christobel Lakey was because he didn't want to alert her husband. The other was because of the cunning plan he had formulated when he had sat simmering on his own property.

He now moved towards the cowshed. Lakey was still in there milking the last of the cows, sitting on a stool, his back to Bayly. Bayly crept forward on the unsuspecting Lakey. Then did he shoot him or strike him? No one heard a gunshot that afternoon, so perhaps he killed him silently.

The next morning he had returned to collect Lakey's wheeled frame and put his body on it. He had wheeled it across to the boundary fence where he had transferred it to his sledge. From there, it had gone into the 44-gallon drum.

As the morbid pall of smoke rose over his property, Bayly returned to the Lakey farm. Passing the body of Christobel Lakey on the ground, he covered it with sackcloths so it would not be discovered too soon by a passerby along the road.

Then he went to the Lakey household and took the rifles,

burying them at the bottom of the lake. He also took a set of Lakey's clothes. His plan was to make it seem as if the couple had had a domestic argument. Then, in a fit of anger, Samuel Lakey had struck out and killed his wife. In guilt or desperation, he had fled. The fact that he had "taken" his rifles with him also made him appear a fugitive from justice and someone who had to be hunted with caution.

But then the crime was discovered faster than Bayly had anticipated because of the sharp eyes of two farmers. He had to hurry to dispose of the evidence, knowing that the police were already searching next door. His mind began to unravel as he sought to dispose of Lakey's watch, giving silent testimony against himself at each part of his property that he tried to secrete some seemingly insignificant part of it.

It was a mind that had once thought coldly and calmly about two murders he had expected to get away with. His arrogance that he would get away with it was based on the experience that he had got away with similar crimes not once, but twice before.

On 29 July 1926, when he was aged 20, Bayly was acquitted at the Auckland Supreme Court on a charge of carnal knowledge.

And then there was that night so long ago now when he had taken the train to visit little Elsie who admired him so. They had met in the garage where there was no one around. They had kissed. But she didn't want to go further, so he suggested they elope to Auckland. They took the Whippet and drove off.

Along the way he had stopped and in the cramped confines of the car had tried to rekindle the physical intimacy he sought from her. He was rough and hurried in his attempt to achieve sexual fulfilment, which he did, after a fashion. But before, during or after, she struck her head accidentally. Just a light blow, but in a moment she was dead.

In a panic, he drove on to Auckland. He drove to College

Rd, Panmure, and carried her 200 yards into the scrub. No doubt she would be found there in a few days.

Then he abandoned the car in Papatoetoe and walked through the night back to his boarding house.

The preceding is conjecture. There is still no evidence to categorically state the man was William Bayly. But there definitely was a man. That is clear from the fact discovered at the post mortem that Elsie had seminal stains on the outside of her underpants. Today the whole matter would have been resolved by a DNA test.

There were many strange twists in the Bayly case. Samuel Lakey had survived a war yet been killed in a supposedly peaceful rural setting. His wife was killed in a pond that she had specially built because of her love of animals. Elsie Walker always wanted to see the bright lights of Auckland, but all she saw of it was darkness and death. William Bayly was convicted of a crime that maybe he should not have been able to commit because he should already have been hanged for another one – the murder of Elsie Walker.

But that is all irrelevant now, for in the case of Elsie Walker, the official verdict is that it is unsolved.

2. James Patrick Ward

A Perfect Murder?

James Patrick Ward was a 63-year-old lawyer who practised from chambers at Security Buildings at 111 Stuart St, Dunedin. In February 1962, a man came to him about a traffic conviction. Ward planned to make an appeal on his behalf.

On 5 February, Ward discussed the appeal with Owen Clement Toomey, who had been a partner at the firm since 1951. Ward was confident of winning the case for his client and he remarked humorously to his partner, "I'll win this appeal unless I get a bomb in the morning mail." Both men had laughed but, tragically, no truer word was ever spoken in jest.

Before he left the office that afternoon, as was his habit, Ward meticulously tidied his desk. All matters requiring his urgent attention were put aside for the following day in one container, incoming mail was put in another pile and all loose files were stored away. Only when the desk was clear and organised did he return home to his wife and an evening of relaxation.

The next morning, Toomey and the office junior, Betty Helen Taylor, arrived at the office before Ward. Taylor had worked for the firm since January 1960 and one of her duties was to pick up the morning mail. That morning she collected it from the Dunedin Chief Post Office shortly before 8.30 am. Inside the postal box was a card for a parcel which had been too large to fit into the postal box.

Taylor took the card to the counter and was presented with a parcel which measured about 25cm wide by 15cm deep by 5cm high. It was surrounded by brown wrapping and addressed to "James Ward & Co" in handwriting.

Taylor took the parcel and the rest of the mail back to the office and gave it to Toomey, who started to open it. One letter was to Ward from his son the Rev Brother Maurice Ward, who was in Australia, so Toomey put that aside. He had started to pull off the outside layer of the wrapping of the brown parcel when he saw there was a second layer underneath that was addressed to Ward and marked "personal". So he put the parcel aside also to await Ward's arrival in the office.

It was not long before Ward came. The two men exchanged the normal pleasantries and Toomey gave Ward his mail. Ward took it, glancing at the parcel with curiosity. As he moved towards his office, the phone rang and he hurried into his room to answer it.

He left the parcel on his desk and when he had finished the call he began to open it.

About three minutes after Ward went into his office, the four-storey building was rocked by a tremendous explosion.

At first Toomey, who was in his office attending to his

morning mail, thought the main office switchboard in the corridor had been blown out. "I left the main office and walked into the corridor," he said in a statement later. "I saw Mr Ward's office was closed. This was unusual. I went to the office and opened the door. I was immediately met by a smell like gunpowder and I saw the room was in a state of chaos."

Ward was lying on the floor on his right side, underneath the two windows that looked out over Stuart St. He was unconscious but still alive. Toomey hurried over to him, bent down and supported his head. Only then did he notice that Ward's left hand had been blown completely off.

Ward had also suffered severe injuries to his chest. As Toomey raised Ward's head, the injured man regained consciousness and tried to focus his eyes. Though Ward was able to address Toomey by his first name, he was disoriented and unsure what had happened. Ward kept requesting that his head be raised and his clothing loosened. Over and over again, he asked what had happened and muttered weakly but audibly, "Who could have done this to me?"

In the main office, Taylor phoned an ambulance. She brought a wet sponge and Toomey tried to soothe his ailing partner by sponging his face with water until the ambulance arrived. Ward asked for morphine.

When the ambulance arrived, Toomey accompanied Ward in it to the hospital. It was only at this point that Toomey realised that it was the parcel that he had given to Ward which had exploded.

At Dunedin Public Hospital, Ward was attended to by the resident surgical officer, Michael Elliott Shackleton, and by John Borrie, senior thoracic surgeon. Ward was able to talk on his arrival at the hospital, but was encouraged by the medical staff to remain quiet. He was operated on immediately and at first it looked as if he might survive. Though he had lost a lot of blood, his heartbeat was still strong, but slowly it faded over the next six hours until he died at 3.15 that afternoon.

By that time, Ward's office had been sealed off by police and a strict ban had been imposed on the press taking photographs of the wrecked office until the forensic experts had completed their investigation. A 24-hour guard was posted to prevent any interference with the murder scene.

Ward's once-neat office presented a picture of utter devastation. One of the office windows had been completely blown away, including the frame, while the glass in the other had been blown out. Ward's antique desk was destroyed while one wall of legal books was a charred mess. The blast had even stripped plaster off the walls back to the laths.

It appeared from the position of Ward's body and the effects of the damage that he had been standing when he opened the parcel. In some small way, the phone may have contributed to his death. Rushing into his office to answer it, Ward was likely to have dropped the parcel onto the desk and snatched up the phone without first taking his seat. Once he had finished the call, still standing, he may have turned his attention to the parcel, probably intrigued by what was inside.

He may well have been leaning over the parcel as he unwrapped it, allowing the full force of the blast to penetrate his chest and spatter blood all over his face.

Had he been sitting at his desk when the bomb exploded, the desk might have protected the lower half of his body from the blast and the injuries to his upper half might have been less severe.

Painstakingly, the police began to sift through the wreckage of the office for clues and the components of the bomb. They found it had been constructed inside a roughly made wooden box.

Part of the box survived the explosion. On the piece of wood were nine blobs of black ink. The ink marks were thought to be part of a stencil painted on the box. The detectives extrapolated that, when fully formed, the

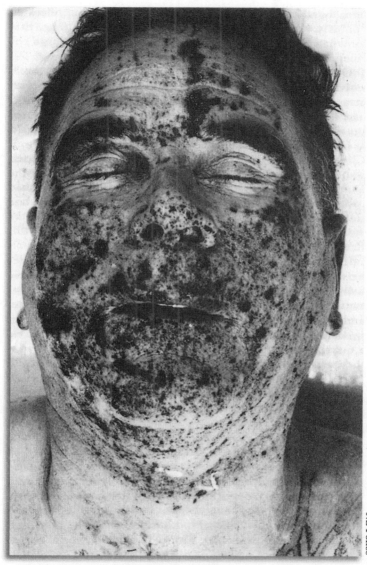

NZ Police

James ward after the bomb in the morning mail.

stencilled letters would read "4PI", and "OO", as well as the vertical stroke of another undecipherable letter.

The police sought a box with similar stencilling to try to determine its origin. Detectives visited two paint warehouses in Dunedin where they lifted boxes and measured stencils for over an hour. The individual stencils used on the paint boxes were almost identical to those on the bomb box but they could not find an identical sequence or one that even looked like the sequence on the bomb box.

The box appeared to be constructed of timber used for packing fruit and paint on the framework was found to contain red colouring. This was unusual, but it did not lead to any new line of inquiry.

Various items including electric wiring and tin were recovered from the debris and pieced together by explosives experts. They concluded that the ignition for the device was generated by two small batteries that would have fitted inside a household torch. These were connected to a pull switch linked to an electronic detonator, which ignited a quantity of explosive that the experts thought was probably three sticks of gelignite.

Although all the known dealers of explosives in the country were questioned, no leads came to light.

It appeared that the action of opening the parcel had completed an electrical circuit, which had detonated the explosive. The switch was identified as one manufactured by a German company, Busch-Jaegar. However, Busch-Jaegar switches were commonly available in New Zealand at the time.

The switch had been sold by a Dunedin electrical store but none of the staff who worked in the shop could recall the sale or the man who had bought it.

As with any bombing, expert opinion varies about the knowledge required to manufacture a bomb. Almost anybody with a passing knowledge of electrical circuits and how to apply them could manufacture one. The real trick is for the constructor not to blow himself up by his own bomb.

In the case of James Ward, the bomber probably attached the inside wrapping of the parcel to the pull switch. As the wrapping was torn away from the parcel, it would have pulled away the switch and triggered the mechanism.

If the parcel had been neatly cut open with scissors, it is possible that the device might not have been activated. However, even if a person starts the tear with scissors or a knife, most people will finish by tearing the wrapping off a loosely wrapped parcel. Did these calculations go through the cunning mind of the bomber as he prepared his device? Could that explain why he took the trouble to wrap the parcel twice?

It is probable that Ward used his right hand to tear away the wrapping and it was his left hand, which was holding the parcel to steady it, which was therefore blown away.

Fortunately for the investigators, the first wrapping had been torn off the parcel by Owen Toomey and had not been destroyed by the explosion, but was in his wastepaper basket. The police had intended to keep this fact quiet, hoping the murderer would relax his guard under the impression he had committed the perfect crime, but they were disappointed when news of the wrapping was leaked to the press.

The wrapping was addressed in clear script and postmarked in Dunedin on the preceding weekend. The wrapping was shown to mailroom officers at the Chief Post Office. None of the post office workers interviewed remembered handling the parcel.

Attempts were made to find latent fingerprints on the wrapping and remains of the bomb parcel, but none were found.

Handwriting experts were brought in to identify the script on the wrapping. At first they believed the wide-handed scrawl to be that of two people who were both attempting to disguise their own style of writing.

The words "James Ward & Co" were written in an untidy "scratchy" style. On the second line, "Security Buildings", the individual letters were spaced further apart and were more rounded, while on the third line, "111 Stuart Street", the writing became tightly cramped.

Finally, they concluded that the writing belonged to just one person. Though the writing could possibly still have been disguised, the experts still felt confident enough to conclude that the writing was the product of "an above-average, educated man".

The police went though many of Ward's documents and business papers to try and match the handwriting found in the files to that on the bomb. The firm's trust account and all business relationships were also investigated to see who could have held such a grudge against him that they would send a bomb.

It soon became clear that Ward had not been well liked. A picture began to emerge of a man who, though a competent lawyer, was pompous and arrogant. Ward was known as a man who always got his way – a tenacious cross-examiner in court who never let up until he got the answer he wanted.

He was also a staunch Roman Catholic and was president of the local St Vincent de Paul Society. Because of his religious convictions, he took strong moral stances on a number of issues and was not slow in forcing his opinion on others.

Because of those religious convictions, he refused to handle divorce actions in his legal work or even disputes between husbands and wives. However, he did represent women in cases where their husbands had abandoned them and was well known for his unyielding attitude towards defaulting husbands.

Over the years, Ward had received many personal threats, usually for refusing to appear in divorce actions or because of his manner in dealing with people.

At that time, a series of anonymous threatening letters had been sent to various people in Dunedin. One such letter had been received by a prominent Roman Catholic who handed it to the police. The letter claimed Roman Catholics were trying to take over the world, and demanded money. The writer was apprehended and admitted that he had sent it. He was accused of demanding money with menaces and appeared in Dunedin High Court on 11 June 1961. However, the police could find no evidence to connect him with the death of James Ward.

Another theory was that the murderer was a Communist. Ward had vociferously attacked communism in the past because of its anti-religious sentiments.

Ward's curious comment to his partner on the day before the tragedy also aroused suspicion. Was he aware of what might occur when he had said that, or was his humour the result of some bizarre psychic intuition? There was no evidence that he had received any threat to his life before the incident. He had said nothing to his wife or anybody else in the firm and no evidence of any threat received was found in his paperwork.

The police began to focus on a particular suspect, who they considered had both the experience and the skill to devise a bomb similar to the one that had killed Ward. The suspect was asked to write out the same wording that had appeared on the parcel.

When the experts analysed the results, they decided that the writing was that of a different man. In this case, it appears the police placed far too much emphasis on expert opinion. Someone who was cunning enough to build a bomb would certainly be cunning enough to disguise their own writing on the package.

While by the nature of their profession many lawyers have been attacked and threatened, Ward was the first in New Zealand to be murdered.

So was it the perfect crime? It could be said that it was, because the perpetrator was never caught and he is unlikely to be identified now. At the time, the police stated, "In our reckoning, there is only one type of perfect crime – and that is when the crime is never discovered."

So this crime was almost perfect as neither the murderer nor his motive was discovered. Yet the killer could easily have been caught. He could have been identified when he took the parcel to the post office and when he bought the switch – but he wasn't.

Luck meant the murderer has probably taken the secret of his deed and his dark motives to his own grave.

3. Jennifer Mary Beard

In the Heat of the Day

The Jennifer Beard case is one of the most notorious unsolved crimes in New Zealand's history. It is also a watershed crime in that it marks the time when a nation lost its innocence.

A few decades before the events that were to take place in Haast Pass, there is a story about a young boy from Auckland who was sent to camp in the south of the North Island. The young boy tired of the camp routine and decided to walk home – all the way to Auckland!

A little way along the road, a car stopped and he was

asked if he wanted a lift. He told the people in the car he was going to Auckland. They said they were too. The boy got in and, to his parents' amazement, walked into the family home in Auckland some hours later.

It is unlikely that could happen today. The climate has changed too much and the Jennifer Beard case was the crime that changed it.

Though many atrocious crimes had been committed before in New Zealand, this was the first murder of a tourist. One who, by all accounts, was friendly and undeserving of her fate, especially on a hot, sunny day in the idyllic South Island at a time when the rest of the country was celebrating the long, leisurely summer holidays.

Jennifer Beard (generally known as Jenny) is usually referred to as a Tasmanian, but she had been living in that part of the world only for the last seven of her 25 years.

In fact, Jennifer Mary Beard was born in Wales, the daughter of a Methodist minister. After leaving Cardiff University at the age of 18, she emigrated to Hobart, Tasmania, where she had an uncle, the Reverend Dr T. C. Beard. She settled in the country and took up a teaching position at Campbelltown.

Jenny was a very popular person and blessed with a cheerful disposition. She was an active sportsperson, engaging in a variety of activities such as hockey, tennis and athletics. But hiking was her first love. It was through hiking that she met and fell in love with the president of the local hiking club, Reg Williams. Reg had been hiking in New Zealand before and enthused Jenny with the opportunities for travel here.

They decided they would spend their Christmas holidays on a hiking holiday in the South Island. They also decided that when they returned to Australia they would announce their engagement and marry at Easter.

The only barrier to their plans was that Reg had already agreed to lead a climbing party through the Milford

News Media Auckland

The last known photograph of Jennifer Beard, taken a few days before she disappeared.

Sounds. So they arranged to travel separately and meet up again in the Milford Sounds between 5-7 January. Both looked forward to the holiday which seemed to be a harbinger of the rest of their lives together.

Jenny was the first to arrive in New Zealand on 19 December, in the company of a party of climbers. Just an hour or two after she left the home of her uncle, with whom she stayed, he received a telephone call from her parents in Wales giving their blessing to her proposed marriage.

Reg arrived in New Zealand almost a week later on Christmas Day. The two were in touch with each other as they went about their different itineraries. As the days passed, Reg looked forward to meeting up with Jenny again as scheduled in Milford on about 5 January. He was disappointed that she did not arrive exactly on that day but he reckoned that she must be enjoying herself and he would simply wait the extra day or two, which was within the time limit they had agreed.

He started to be concerned when she had not arrived by the evening of the 7th. It was so unlike her. He knew that her itinerary had included passing through Wanaka and then going south to Queenstown, Te Anau and on to Milford. She had planned to be in Wanaka on 1 January to pick up her mail. But when he checked with the Wanaka Post Office, he found that her mail was still unclaimed.

He contacted the climbing party she had accompanied and was told that she had last been seen heading towards the Franz Josef Glacier. She had not been heard of since. Every day, Reg waited for Jenny, hoping that would be the day he saw her smiling face. But she never came. Finally on 11 January, knowing that something was dreadfully wrong, he went to the police and reported Jenny as a missing person.

The officer in charge of the investigation was Detective Inspector Emmett T. Mitten. He immediately initiated a sweeping search for Jenny concentrating on the area between Franz Josef Glacier and Wanaka. It was not easy ground to search. The area was sparsely populated and the rugged terrain was sliced through by many fast-flowing rivers.

At first, the search was conducted by 30 police officers, who worked long hours without any extra pay (the police don't get overtime, they get leave credited against the extra hours they put in during a major investigation). During the search for Jenny, a normal day started about 7.30 am and was likely to finish about 1.30 am the following day.

Based at Lake Moeraki, they were completely cut off from civilisation. Lake Moeraki is at the end of the telephone line from the north. In order to call Haast, which was only 40km away, the call had to go back over the Alps to Christchurch, down to Dunedin and back over to the West Coast and then down to Haast.

Even when the connection was made, reception was very poor. Voices were faint and men using the line had to shout to be heard. Nor for the first few days were the police officers allowed any contact with their families because the single telephone line had to be used 24 hours a day for teleprinter and police work.

Radio contact was also limited because of the surrounding mountains.

After six days without result, 51 soldiers kitted out with camping gear were called in. Five more policemen were added, which brought the total number of searchers to 86. They kept at it, hoping they would find Jenny somewhere in this inhospitable terrain, yet at the same time they were hoping they wouldn't find her.

Photographs of Jenny were published in newspapers and the police invited people who had given her lifts to come forward. Slowly, the police were able to piece together her last known movements. But as they did so another indelible image began to form. The nation conceived a picture of the personality of Jenny herself from the words of those who had come into contact with her during the brief time she had been in New Zealand.

On 29 December, a Nelson couple had given Jenny a lift from Springfield to Arthur's Pass. They had liked her enough to take photographs of her, which they later sent to her uncle, Reverend Dr T. C. Beard, who had flown over from Australia.

The Nelson couple had got on so well with Jenny that they had offered to take her all the way to Haast Pass. Perhaps it would have saved her life if she had accepted, but she declined. Instead she spent the night with them at a motor camp and the next morning they dropped her off at Arthur's Pass.

Later the wife wrote to Jenny's relatives, "Jenny was one of the most lovable people we have ever met. "Her husband wrote, "In the short time we were privileged to be with her, she made a very favourable impression on us and it was with considerable reluctance that I did not agree to my wife's suggestion that we should change our entire holiday plans and continue right down the coast and through Haast. She was keen to do this so that we could show Jenny all of our adopted country, for we are also from Britain.

"However, we went through that area only two years ago and had planned this year to spend several days each at Arthur's Pass and Mt Cook. We first met Jenny just west of Springfield and soon established mutual interests – our country of origin, our love of exploring, and the fact that our two sons are both training to be teachers.

"We stopped at Lake Lyndon and shared our picnic lunch and on arrival at the pass, which had been our destination, checked with the ranger about camp sites. We invited Jenny to share our camp facilities at Arthur's Pass for she had no independent cooking or toilet facilities.

"She accepted our invitation and became a member of the family, helping in camp chores, sharing the supplies and accompanying us to the park headquarters for a slide evening.

"We suggested to Jenny that she might join us in exploring on foot for a day, but after studying our maps and hearing our description of the route ahead, she decided to press on her way.

"We had a reasonably early breakfast and after she had packed her gear we took her further up the road to the top of the pass, where I had planned to leave her at a convenient spot for further lifts. However my wife was so persuasive that eventually we drove down the gorge."

They said that when they left her, Jenny was carrying a very heavy rucksack and a camera. She had told them that after Arthur's Pass she intended to go through the Otira Gorge.

Three families from Dunedin who were holidaying together, named Sonntag, Kindley, and McIlroy, also spoke to Jenny at Franz Josef motor camp. She told them of her plans to go through Wanaka and then to meet up with her fiancé in Milford Sound.

The next morning she was seen heading south from the camp. The Kindleys, Sonntags and the McIlroys also left the camp that morning, travelling in convoy towards Wanaka. At one point, they became separated and the Sonntags travelled alone while the other two families travelled together, though they also parted at times.

At about 10 am, the McIlroys arrived at Fox Glacier. Mrs McIlroy saw Jenny sitting in the front passenger seat of a car with a man in the driver's seat. She saw Jenny get out of the car and take a photograph of the glacier. Jenny was wearing shorts and tramping boots.

The car which Jenny was in left first and headed south. The McIlroys also left the glacier heading south and at a point on the road overtook the car with Jenny in it.

The Kindleys also passed the car and Mrs Kindley recognised Jenny sitting in the passenger seat. The Kindleys stopped at a deer farm along the road and while they were there again saw the car drive past them with Jenny in the passenger seat. It was still travelling south at a steady speed of about 70km/h.

The Kindleys continued south and travelling at a faster

speed once more caught up with and overtook the car. Near Lake Paringa, the Kindleys stopped to assist at the scene of a motor accident. There, they again saw the car with Jenny in it pass them.

The Kindleys then continued driving south toward Lake Moeraki. Just before reaching the Moeraki River Bridge, they again passed the car. They turned off the road to stop at a tearooms and their last sighting of the car Jenny was in was as it drove south over the Moeraki River Bridge. It was travelling very slowly. The time was about 12.30 pm.

A family from Dunedin, the Crossans, was crossing the Moeraki River Bridge at about the same time. They passed a green Vauxhall car, 1954-55 model. One of the family saw a young woman in the car. He could not say if it was Jennifer Beard but when he waved at her she cheerfully waved back.

The sighting that the police saw as the most reliable, however, was that of a 13-year-old boy from Timaru. His family had been travelling along the same stretch of road on 31 December when their car approached a Vauxhall with its bonnet up by the side of the road.

The boy said that a middle-aged, balding and overweight man was leaning underneath the bonnet apparently trying to repair the engine. His father brought their car to a halt beside the Vauxhall and offered to help. The man declined assistance.

As the man leant over the engine, his shirt rode up his back and the boy said later that he had the hairiest back he had ever seen, almost like a gorilla's. The boy and his father paid little attention to the person sitting in the passenger seat. All they remembered was that it was a woman.

At about 1.17 pm on 31 December, the Crossans stopped at a rest area at the northern end of the Haast River Bridge. They saw a man apparently having trouble with a car similar to the one the Kindleys had seen Miss Beard in. Mr Crossan helped the man to get the car mobile.

Based on this information from the Crossan family, on

News Media Auckland

Police search for evidence in the Haast River
near where Jennifer Beard was found.

15 January the search party moved to the area of the Haast River Bridge near to where the boy had seen the man with a "back like a gorilla". They moved in formation through the scrub around the bridge. Detective Senior Sergeant Joy was moving forward under the last span of the northern side of the bridge when he came across a female body which was partially hidden by bushes.

It was the body of Jennifer Beard, lying on her back in an advanced state of decomposition. The left arm was extended outward, with the forearm, which had no flesh on it, lying over her face, as if while still alive she had been attempting to defend herself.

Jenny had been wearing three pairs of pants. These had been neatly rolled down to her knees.

An extremely discoloured reddish tartan shirt was pushed up towards the neck, twisted across the junction of the upper and lower two-thirds of the arm. The sleeves of the shirt had been turned inside out. Four buttons were missing from the front of the shirt and at least three of these appeared to have been wrenched off, tearing the cloth. There was a 30cm tear up the body of the shirt and a 26cm tear down the inside of the right arm.

It was as if someone had forced the shirt up around her neck. Her bra had also been pushed up without bothering to undo the fastening.

From the shorts that had been neatly pulled down to below Jenny's knees, it seemed she had gone under the bridge to relieve herself. By the way the clothes of her upper body appeared to have been hurriedly thrust aside, it seemed she had been interrupted by someone who had awkwardly and brutally sexually assaulted her.

As her body remained in the same place, it could be assumed that she had died during the attack and was left there. The Government analyst made a detailed study of the area. A number of footprints were similar to the pattern of Jenny's tramping boots, but there were other footprints in the area.

On the bank, he discovered that some small tender gorse bushes had been pulled out by their roots. This was consistent with someone having scrambled up the bank in a mad haste.

Police attention now focussed on the last car she had been seen in, the Vauxhall. The 13-year-old boy had described the car as a 1953-55 Vauxhall with the bodywork in good condition. Many people claimed to have seen the car but the description of it varied from person to person. The colour ranged from light chocolate to turquoise, and the condition from well maintained to in need of painting.

With the many conflicting reports, the police paid more attention to the description of the 13-year-old lad, believing his perception and recall to be superior to that of the adults.

The descriptions of the driver also varied. He was described as thickset, middle-aged and balding. Where many described him as overweight, others said he had a prominent stomach to the point of being pot-bellied.

With the assistance of the various witnesses, an artist drew an identikit picture of him. These were widely publicised and a total of 124 letters were received from people claiming to have seen a man who fitted the description with a female passenger in the area.

About 900 people were also named by people as a result of the pictures. Where possible, these people were traced and eliminated.

The Crossans reported that they had left the rest area by the Haast River Bridge at about 1.30 pm and continued north. Shortly before they reached the Waita River, the Vauxhall which had been in the rest area overtook them. When the Crossans continued north, somewhere between the Moeraki River Bridge and Bruce Bay, they were again overtaken by the car, travelling north at speed.

Why had the car suddenly speeded up? Also it overtook the Crossans on two separate occasions. That means at some point the car must have stopped somewhere and possibly left the road altogether as the Crossan family had not noticed overtaking it.

If the man who drove the car was the killer, he would have taken off at speed after murdering Jenny. Then he would have realised that he still had her backpack and camera in the car. He would know with certainty that these would incriminate him.

He had to detour off the road to try and find somewhere to dispose of them. Then he got back onto the road and got away as fast as his car would take him.

The police made an extensive search for the camera. They were especially eager to find it because the people Jenny had met along the way had noticed that she liked to take a lot of photographs. The police hoped that she had taken a photograph of her murderer and he would be on the film.

A mechanic, Edward Joseph Watson, of the Bruce Bay Store, told the police that, some time after 1 pm that afternoon, a greeny-blue Vauxhall called at the store and he attended to the gear linkages.

At about 3 pm that same day, a Vauxhall of similar description called at Arnold Motors at Fox Glacier to have faulty linkages remedied.

In the middle of the afternoon of 31 December, another mechanic, Harold Pratt, told the police that early that afternoon a Vauxhall car was driven to his garage at Haast and he was asked to attend to the gear linkages. Pratt described the driver as being pot-bellied. He said the man had a definite paunch overhanging the belt of his trousers.

The police continued the search for the car, realising that if they found it they would be able to find the driver. Earlier, a tourist had actually taken a picture of the Haast River Bridge with a Vauxhall crossing it. Was it the Vauxhall the police were seeking? They would never know as the numberplate of the car was obscured.

Another man had noted the registration number of the wanted car. But then he had lost it!

News Media Auckland

The Identikit picture of the man it is believed
murdered Jennifer Beard.

The police were also searching for four men who had separately signed into West Coast motor camps about the time of the murder. The men, named Scott, Horan, Norris and Oldfield, could have been staying in the motels under assumed names. In each of the four places, people had said there was a green Vauxhall car present. None of the men was located.

A Gisborne couple came forward and said they had met someone who had travelled with Jenny. They said her name was Miss Rose Moore and she was a Scottish schoolteacher. She had travelled with Jenny and a middle-aged man. She may have been able to provide vital evidence but, despite appeals, no Miss Moore came forward.

As in any investigation, there were a number of likely suspects. By eliminating the most unlikely, the police narrowed it down to just one man. He drove a Vauxhall car, was middle-aged and had a stout build that could have been interpreted as being overweight. He had been on the Haast Pass road at about that time, having left his house early that morning to go on a fishing trip.

The man went to the local police station, where he remained for five hours being interviewed by Detective Inspector Mitten and a colleague. His Vauxhall was collected from his house in the south-east area of Timaru that night and taken to Timaru Police Station.

That same night, four witnesses were taken to Timaru and boarded in a city hotel.

Early the next morning, the Vauxhall was closely examined by detectives and forensic experts. Photographs were taken of the exterior and interior of the vehicle. This vehicle was then placed with nine other Vauxhalls in two rows. The drivers of the cars, nine men and a woman, then stood by their cars as the witnesses – three men and a young girl – walked along the row of cars accompanied by two detectives. The drivers were then asked to leave their vehicles while witnesses examined the cars.

Bonnets were raised as one of the witnesses, who was

presumably a mechanic, made an inspection of gear linkage mechanisms. The windscreens and left side of the front fenders of the vehicles were also closely inspected by this witness.

No material evidence eventuated from it sufficient to warrant charging the suspect with the crime.

The body of Jennifer Mary Beard was cremated in Christchurch on 24 January 1970 at the request of her parents. The sole mourner was her uncle, Reverend Dr T. C. Beard.

As the cremation service was taking place, Jenny's family held a simultaneous private service of prayer in her home of Hawarden, Wales, where Jenny's father was the Methodist minister.

A year after the murder, a team of 13 policemen and legal advisers again checked the evidence. The chief suspect was again taken to Timaru Police Station and interviewed. Later, detectives twice called at his house to talk to him personally. The assembled officers could not agree on whether to charge the suspect. Finally, it was decided that the evidence was insufficient to press charges. It was not a view shared by investigating officer Mitten. "I believed at the meeting we had sufficient evidence to prove a charge of murder," he said later.

An inquest was held on 10 August 1971 at which the coroner, Mr R. M. Vincent, found that Jennifer Beard died of unknown causes, adding: "From the evidence... I also note from the disarrayed clothing and the fact Miss Beard's effects were never found, that it leaves no doubt that another person had been implicated in this death. I am satisfied Miss Beard was murdered by the man driving the Vauxhall who was seen in the rest area at Haast, but at this stage there has been insufficient evidence to charge any person with the murder of Jennifer Mary Beard."

He said that the unsatisfactory conclusion to the investigation resulted from the 11 days that had elapsed between the time of Jenny's disappearance and the reporting of her to the police as missing. But Jenny's body had actually been found even before she was reported missing.

On 3 January 1970, a family of five was crossing the Haast River Bridge when an 8-year-old girl told her parents she needed to go to the toilet. The car was stopped in the rest area and she headed for the privacy of the bushes underneath the bridge. When she came back a few minutes later, she said: "Daddy, there's a lady lying near the stream. She hasn't got any clothes on. I think she is asleep."

It is possible her father did not believe her, but he certainly did not investigate. If only he had believed the word of a child.

A reward of $5000 was offered for information leading to the arrest and conviction of Jenny's murderer. The police inquiries were extensive and people were interviewed as far away as Japan and Britain. In all, about 50,000 people were interviewed and about 14,800 Vauxhalls were inspected out of the 35,000 then registered in New Zealand, but the police were unable to track down the murderer.

In 1988, 18 years after Jenny's death, there was an unusual development when the man who had been the key suspect in the case came forward and spoke to his local paper, the Timaru Herald.

Gordon Joseph Bray was then aged 70 years and still a bachelor. He was a big-boned man with thick-rimmed glasses. He was powerfully built, with strong arm muscles that came from many years working as a truck driver, demolition man, labourer and drainlayer. He had lived all his life in South Canterbury, most of it in the small, weathered, wooden house he shared with his middle-aged brother and sister.

He had been on holiday in South Westland for 10 days when Jennifer Beard disappeared. On the actual day she disappeared, he said he had been in the Forks area, "fishing and poking about".

He said he had gone through the Haast region the day

before Jennifer Beard was believed to have been murdered. He had crossed the Haast River Bridge but had not stopped, slowing down a little to see how much water was in the river, so that he could assess its prospects for trout fishing. He had decided not to stop.

The police had asked him to assist with inquiries after he returned to work. They took away his 1954 Vauxhall Velox, painted a deep blue, and searched it for clues. The police, he said, were looking for a green one.

Bray said police took him under escort to South Westland where they asked him to retrace the steps of his 10-day holiday. They also took him to the exact spot where Jenny's body was found beneath the Haast River Bridge.

At one of two police identification parades in Timaru, he was picked out by the 13-year-old boy, but Bray said the identification parades were "hopelessly at variance". The people picked out ranged by between four stone in weight and six inches in height.

"A bloke standing next to me was picked twice and a bloke who worked with me once on the Canterbury Power Board was also picked. They brought a joker over from the Fox River and he picked two different men."

Bray was nearly killed one Sunday evening in September 1976 when he was knocked down by a car on a pedestrian crossing outside the Timaru Chief Post Office. He suffered severe head injuries, lacerations, a broken right leg and internal injuries. He had total memory loss for several weeks after the accident but said there was no truth in the rumours that the police had stayed up all night with him after the accident awaiting a death-bed confession.

Years later, one of the forensic experts involved in the case expressed his dissatisfaction with the theory that Jenny had been murdered. Pat Alcorn had worked for the Department of Scientific and Industrial Research (DSIR) for 41 years and had handled hundreds of cases involving minute research and detection work but none of them troubled him as much as Jenny's case.

He was one of the men who had carried her body out from under the bridge. Because of the amount of decomposition, no hyoid bone was found. The hyoid bone is a U-shaped, cartilaginous bone situated at the base of the tongue and the top of the throat. It would have to be inspected for a case of strangulation to be proved.

When they were carrying the body away from the area, Alcorn noticed large dragonflies in the vicinity. He believed that Jennifer Beard had gone down to the bridge to go to the toilet and had been spooked by the insects. When one of them got inside her blouse, she panicked and, while hurriedly pulling aside her blouse to try and get it out, she swallowed her tongue and suffocated.

The driver of the car who was waiting on top of the bridge would have wondered why she was taking so long. When he found her dead, he would have realised that he would now be the chief suspect in a murder inquiry and he would have hurried away.

It seems unlikely that Jenny could be killed by a dragonfly. The far more likely scenario was that she was killed by the middle-aged man who drove the Vauxhall.

When he was driving along and saw the pretty girl with the slim figure hitching beside the road did some long-forgotten yearnings stir within him?

As they drove along those long country roads on that hot day, it seems certain that Jenny would have engaged him in friendly conversation. Did he misinterpret her smiles and her laughter? Did her bare legs within touching distance of his clumsy hands incite feelings that he barely managed to restrain?

He had been driving his car slowly because he knew there were problems with it. It had played up, forcing a stop at the Moeraki River Bridge. It still didn't seem right as he approached the Haast River Bridge, so he pulled over into the rest area and lifted the bonnet again.

Jenny sat in the passenger seat of the car waiting patiently. When others stopped to try to help him fix the car she was too polite to suggest that perhaps she might carry on with them. Instead, she was loyal to the man who had given her a lift, the man who would cut short her life.

After a while, she felt the urge to go to the toilet and realised it would be a good time with the car stopped. She told the driver. He nodded. She trusted him enough to leave her rucksack and camera in his car.

But she did not see his gaze follow her as she disappeared into the bushes. The man probably hesitated. He knew he was stepping over an invisible line. He knew she might refuse his advances. Then he followed her.

Underneath the bridge, Jenny glanced about to check she had privacy, then she tidily rolled down her three pairs of shorts and squatted to perform her call of nature.

She was a churchgoer and had very high moral principles. It was also likely she was a virgin. She probably had no idea at all what was going on in the driver's mind.

He followed her footsteps quickly but quietly. Intent on what she was doing, she was at her most vulnerable. He probably attacked her from behind, pushing her to the ground, and before she could get up, held her down and roughly pulled away her blouse and bra.

Then what happened? Why did she die? There was no clear evidence that she was strangled. So why did her breathing stop? Did her attacker murder her or was the attack so barbarous and so treacherous to her own generous nature that she simply died of shock?

Then realising what he had done, the driver scrambled in a panic back up the bank. He would have raced away at speed, forgetting that her bag and camera were still in the car. When he realised, he might have considered returning to place them beside the body.

But that was too dangerous. Instead he drove on northwards, overtaking the Crossans. When there were no other cars around, somewhere between the Waita Bridge and Paringa, he went off down a side road. He was in wild terrain of dense native bush, swamps, ravines and swift-flowing rivers that swept into the sea. There are many places to hide a rucksack and camera.

Then he returned to the road, and the car that had been doing 70km/h with Jenny in it now went fast enough to overtake the Crossans once more.

The old car couldn't take it and twice he had to call in at garages to get the gear linkages attended to. Then he was back on the road. He kept driving, driving along the long, lonely country road. He kept driving until he was gone.

4. David Harvey Crewe & Jeanette Lenore Crewe

Who Really Killed the Crewes?

The double murder of Harvey and Jeannette Crewe is probably the most notorious unsolved murder in New Zealand's history. It led to this country's longest-running legal saga and the fallout harmed many more lives than just those of the original two victims. It was also a textbook case in how not to conduct an investigation.

The murders took place in the rural community of Pukekawa about 70km south of Auckland. Another murder occurred in that same region in 1920 that had similarities to the later case.

On the night of 24 August 1920, Sydney Seymour Eyre

and his wife were asleep in their separate beds in their farmhouse at Pukekawa when, at about 11 pm, Mrs Eyre was awoken by the sound of a dog barking. Soon the barking stopped, so she went back to sleep.

She was shortly awoken by a violent explosion. A few feet away her husband lay dead in his bed. The next morning, the police discovered tracks in the ground which had been softened by the heavy rain that had fallen for several days before the murder. They were able to follow the footsteps of a man who had walked up to the bedroom window of the house. After committing the crime, he had fled on horseback. Those tracks were also clearly imprinted in the mud.

The animal he rode that night had a distinctive gait and had also worn hand-made horseshoes. The tracks were found to match those of a roan colt called Mickey, which was used by a local farmhand called Samuel Thorne.

The detective in charge of the investigation, New Zealand's own Sherlock Holmes James Cummings, soon discovered that Eyre had recently travelled to Canada. While away, Samuel Thorne had worked at the farm and struck up an intimate friendship with Mrs Eyre.

On his return, Eyre realised he was not to enjoy the same relations as before with his wife. He needed a bed to sleep in, so he asked Thorne to assist him to move another bed into the marital bedroom.

The night of the murder, Thorne sneaked up to the window, aimed the gun at where he knew Eyre to be and shot him dead.

Thorne was brought to trial but despite the apparently overwhelming evidence the first jury could not agree. He was convicted at a second trial on 3 December 1920. Thirteen days later, he was executed.

The Thorne case had several bizarre similarities with the murders of Harvey and Jeannette Crewe. Some of them were no doubt because the nature of the farming country of Pukekawa had changed little in the intervening half a century, but other similarities were probably introduced by a police investigation that at times strayed dangerously away from the facts.

Harvey Crewe and the then Jeannette Demler had met when Jeannette went to Wanganui to teach in the mid-1960s. Jeannette was a bridesmaid at a friend's wedding and Harvey was a groomsman. It is not recorded if Jeannette caught the bouquet but romance blossomed from that first meeting.

The couple were married in Auckland in June 1966. Jeannette was the daughter of a farmer and Harvey was employed as a shepherd, so it was inevitable that they would settle down to a life on the land.

Jeannette had been left a half-share in her mother's farm alongside State Highway 22 in Pukekawa. Harvey took a mortgage and bought the other half, which had been left to Jeannette's sister Heather. So the newlyweds were able to start their life together on their own farm.

Harvey was a big man who stood about 1.85m tall and weighed about 100kg. He was also said to have a violent temper and there were many instances of his losing it over the years. Before he was married, and when he was working as a shepherd in the Woodville area, he lost his temper with the farmer who was employing him and as a result also lost his job.

On another occasion, he lost it when two stock agents arrived at the Pukekawa farm 10 minutes early for an appointment. When he saw them pull up, Harvey stormed out of the house in his socks, told them they had interrupted his breakfast and instructed them to sit in their car and wait.

On another occasion, he abused some workers who had come to topdress his farm and accused them of submitting inflated bills.

During the four years Harvey and Jeannette spent at Pukekawa, some strange incidents occurred.

On 29 July 1967, their house was burgled. Jewellery

was taken including a sterling silver brush and comb set (which was to feature later in the trials). Strangely, other valuable items such as money and Harvey Crewe's gun were overlooked by the thieves.

In about December 1968, there was a mysterious fire at the house and in June 1969 the haybarn went up in flames. As a result, Jeannette became nervous and would not stay in the house on her own. When Harvey went to work in the fields, she would sit nearby in the car waiting for him.

Apart from these odd events, the Crewes seemed to be a normal, hard-working farming couple. Their daughter Rochelle was born in December 1968 and Jeannette's father, Len Demler, who lived on the adjoining farm, visited the couple and his granddaughter regularly.

On 22 June 1970, Len Demler received a phone call from a local stock agent, Ron Wright, who wanted to send trucks to the Crewe farm to pick up sheep, but he could get no answer on the phone. He had already received a similar call from another stock agent, Jerry Moore, who had gone to the farm himself but could also find no sign of the Crewes. After the second phone call, Demler decided to investigate.

He parked his car on the road and went through the gate into the front paddock which led to the house. He walked through it past the milling sheep to the gate that led to the house. As he approached the house, he could hear Rochelle talking to herself.

He went around to the back of the house where, despite the fact that it was the middle of the day, the back light had been left on. The key was in the door as usual. He entered the house through the kitchen and saw that light was on as well. On the table was an uneaten meal. He walked on through the house and saw blood on the carpet. That was when he realised something terrible had happened.

He found young Rochelle in her cot. He said she looked very thin and had been crying a lot, though she was not crying at that moment. There was no one else in the house.

Len Demler might have been expected to call the police

The blood-stained Crewe lounge.
Note the long mark where a body has been dragged.

at that point but inexplicably he didn't. Instead, he decided to cancel the stock trucks. He abandoned his 18-month-old granddaughter alone at the scene of what appeared to be a murder and drove back to his own farm. But when he phoned to cancel the trucks, Ron Wright was not in the office. Instead of simply leaving a message, he waited for him to return while his granddaughter remained alone in the Crewe farmhouse.

Even when Demler had spoken to Wright, he still did not

phone the police but went to see a neighbour, Owen Priest, whom he asked to accompany him to the house. Priest did not know what to expect when he walked in and was shocked to see the bloodstains on the carpet. Apprehensively, he searched the house. He went right through to the back of the house, uncertain if there would be anybody lurking behind a doorway. When he was almost at the other end of the house, he turned to make a remark to Demler, who he assumed had followed him in, and found Demler had not gone in at all, but had remained by the back door.

Demler already seemed to know what had happened, saying, "The bugger's killed her and done himself in. I tell you, Harvey's killed her." Finally, Priest told him to shut up. Demler went quiet after that.

They searched outside for the bodies of the Crewes, but when they did not find them they returned to the farmhouse to attend to young Rochelle. Only then did Owen Priest call the police. But before the police investigation team arrived, so did many well-meaning neighbours, wiping out any tyre tracks the murderer might have left in the front paddock.

A police search for the bodies began immediately, utilising the resources of the Army, Navy and Air Force.

From unused newspaper and milk deliveries at the Crewe farmhouse, the police determined the murder had probably occurred on 17 June 1970. Except for possibly the killer or killers, it seemed no one had visited the Crewes for five days. No one realised there was anything wrong or that 18-month-old Rochelle Crewe was alone in the house.

There was, however, evidence that Rochelle had not been alone on the Crewe property during that period. On Friday 19 June, farmhand Bruce Roddick saw a mystery woman standing at the gate. The deliveryman noticed that curtains which were drawn on the Thursday were open the following Monday. At 7.30 am on 19 June, sparks were seen coming from the Crewe chimney.

On the next day at about 1.30 pm, Queenie McConachie was passing the Crewe farmhouse in a car when she saw a child toddle down the front path of the Crewe farmhouse. The child was dressed in identical clothes to those Rochelle was wearing when she was discovered.

If Rochelle Crewe had been fed or attended to during those five days, it could have been done only by the murderer or someone who knew the identity of the murderer. From the extensive bloodstains in the lounge, it appeared the Crewes had been shot there and their bodies removed in a wheelbarrow to some other unknown location. The murderer had attempted to clean up the blood but there were bloodstained saucepans in the kitchen and the murderer had also burnt a hearth mat in the fire, presumably to hide something that incriminated him. The police vacuumed fragments from the carpet searching for clues.

On 7 August, the search, which covered an area of nearly 700 square miles, was called off without any trace of the bodies having been found. Demler was never involved, preferring to leave it to the authorities. During the search, on 6 July, he had a party to celebrate his birthday.

Darkness had fallen on 8 August when Ian and Sarah Spratt saw an eerie sight at the Crewe farm. The lights were on in the farmhouse and somebody was moving about in there. They didn't know who it was, whether the police or the murderer trying to hide some evidence he had just remembered. But they failed to call the police.

The investigation was grinding to a halt when there was a sensational development on 16 August. Jeannette's body was found by two men whitebait fishing at a point known as Devil's Elbow on the Waikato River. It had been wrapped in bedclothes and bound with wire. Her body was dressed in a cardigan, a check shirt, a singlet, a bra, trousers, pantyhose and underpants. She had two small injuries to her right temple, injuries about the right eye and the nose, and small injuries to the face which seemed to have been caused after her death. She had six lower teeth missing. Lodged in her head was the fragment of a .22 bullet. The pathologist was able to determine that the bullet had entered her head on the right-hand side in front of the ear, before exiting in front of the left ear.

Now that they had a fragment of a bullet, the police pursued a new line of inquiry because when a bullet is fired from a gun or rifle, the passage of the bullet along the barrel leaves indentations in the bullet that are unique to that rifle. The police collected 64 rifles of .22 calibre within a 10km radius of the Crewe home for examination.

On the bullet that killed Jeannette Crewe was a number 8. It was discovered this meant that the bullet was one of 158 million made by the manufacturer, ICI, between 1948 and 1963.

Of the 64 rifles tested, the forensic expert Dr Nelson was able to eliminate all but two rifles, though the fragmented nature of the bullet meant it was impossible to definitely prove that either had fired the bullet. It was possible that if other rifles had been tested, some would not have been able to be excluded from the test.

Of the two remaining after the initial test, one belonged to a man called Brewster, while the other belonged to a local farmer, Arthur Allan Thomas.

At the time, as far as the police were concerned, Len Demler was the number one suspect. Later, the police were to attempt to concentrate on sex as a motive, but far more important to the farmer are land, money and stock.

In July 1969, Jeannette's mother and Len's wife, Maisie Demler, changed her will to cut out her daughter Heather, who had married a divorced man and an undischarged bankrupt. Len Demler then changed his will leaving his half of the property to Heather, so the sisters were each due to inherit one half again.

Maisie Demler died on 26 February 1970. The will was probated on 16 March and was available for inspection on 16 June. When Jeannette Crewe went in and inspected it,

A bullet of the type that was used to kill the Crewes.

she might have found out for the first time how much her half-share of the farm her father was running was worth.

If Demler was the murderer, then land undoubtedly was the motive. Jeannette – and therefore Harvey – owned a half-share of his farm, and for the first time they realised what it was worth. The police believed that Harvey had told Demler he wanted to buy him out.

There was also the matter of the stock. If Jeannette owned half the farm, she also owned half the stock, so Harvey might have a say when Demler took animals to stock sales, and he might also want half of the proceeds.

On the night of 17 June 1970, it is possible that Demler visited Harvey and Jeannette. There was an argument, Harvey lost his temper and Demler stormed out. While Harvey sat down in his chair to read the paper, Demler went back to his farm and got his gun.

As usual, the key was in the back door of the Crewe house when he returned. He came in quietly. He didn't want to alert Harvey, as Harvey was stronger than him.

When Demler came around the kitchen door, Harvey was sitting in the chair with his back to him. Before Harvey was even aware of his presence, Demler aimed and shot him through the back of the head. A distraught Jeannette rose out of the chair she had been sitting in and started screaming at her father. He struck her in the face and knocked her down, then stood over her and pumped a bullet straight into her head. The bullet exited into the hearth mat, which was why he tried to burn it to hide the mark.

Disturbed by the noise, Rochelle woke up in her cot and started crying. Demler ignored her and left to return to his own house. He knew the bodies would be found and there would be an investigation. The more he thought about it, the more he realised that the police investigation would focus on him.

He lived next door and he had no alibi. The matter of the wills would come out and the police would find no one else with any other motive. There had been no sexual assault, no valuables were missing. In the absence of other suspects, the police searchlight would inevitably point at him.

He returned to the Crewe farmhouse. The two farms were sheltered from each other by bush so he could get to it from the back of his farm without being seen from the road.

He had brought with him the farmer's staple, some number 8 fencing wire. He realised that the bodies would leave less blood on the carpet or in his car if they were wrapped. He took blankets from the Crewe house and then bound the bodies with the wire. Jeannette was lighter and easy to lift, but he had to drag Harvey's body along the carpet. It was only later that he noticed Harvey's body had left bloodstained drag marks across the carpet.

Nor did he notice that blood dripped from Jeannette onto the front seat of his car. Then he drove through darkness to the Waikato River, where he dumped the bodies, having attached weights to them.

Over the next few days, he returned to the Crewe farmhouse and tried to dispose of the evidence, cleaning up the blood and burning the mat.

He fed Rochelle and changed her until the nappies ran out. He also fed the dogs to keep them quiet. He did not move the bottles and newspapers from the front of the house because it was too risky – he might be seen from the road.

Then he stopped going to the house, waiting for someone to discover the murder. But for several days no one did. When the stock agents went to the house, they failed to raise the alarm and phoned him instead. Prompted by that, he pretended to go to the house himself, but in fact went to get neighbour Owen Priest as a "witness".

Only if he were the murderer would it explain his strange actions after "finding" Rochelle. And where was the gun that was recorded in estate papers but which was missing? Had Demler hidden it because it was the murder weapon?

The above scenario is a reconstruction of what the police probably discussed at a conference held on 15 September. The result was that they decided to arrest Len Demler and charge him with the murder of the Crewes.

The next day, a major development changed the course of the inquiry. Harvey Crewe's body was found in the Waikato River, 6km upstream from where Jeannette's body had been found. It was badly decomposed and in danger of breaking up. The police tried to put the body in a cradle but something prevented them. Detective Inspector Hutton, who was in charge of the inquiry, noticed a wire going around the left armpit and stomach of Harvey Crewe's body. He felt underneath and concluded that the object holding the body was made of iron. The object was released and the body freed up.

Hutton ordered the police divers to dive at the spot where the body had been found and the only object they found which fitted what Hutton had described was a car axle. It seemed to Hutton that the wire could have been tied to the kingpin end of the axle.

The axle had been part of a 1929 Nash motorcar. A man called Shirtcliffe said he once owned a trailer which had a 1929 Nash axle on it. He even had a photograph of it. He had sold it in 1958 to Arthur Allan Thomas' father.

In the mid-1960s, an engineer called Rasmussen had modified a trailer for Thomas senior and taken the old 1929 Nash axle off it. Mr Thomas senior had taken it away with him and as far as he knew left it on the farm that Arthur Allan Thomas was now leasing from him.

The police now had two reasons to link Arthur Allan Thomas with the murder of the Crewes and they quickly found a third. Thomas and Jeannette Crewe had known each other since they were children and, when older, Thomas had, by all accounts, been rather keen on Jeannette though they had never gone out together. However Thomas had once been on good enough terms with her to present her with a brush and comb set.

Arthur Allan Thomas now became the prime suspect. The police questioned him on several occasions. He had an alibi for 17 June that could be corroborated only by his wife and a sick cow – which had been calving the night the Crewes were murdered.

Earlier that day, Arthur Allan Thomas and his wife, Vivian, had gone to the dentist at Pukekohe. They arrived home at about 4 pm and Thomas had gone to attend to the sick cow at about 5 pm. They finished calving the cow somewhere between 6 and 7 o'clock and had a late tea. There was a ratepayers' meeting elsewhere in Pukekawa that night. Thomas' aunt invited them to go to it, but they declined and went to bed some time between 9 and 9.30 pm.

The police would later contend that, while Vivian was asleep, Arthur Allan Thomas got out of bed, drove to the Crewe farmhouse, murdered two people, wrapped the bodies in blankets and number 8 wire, drove them to the Waikato River and dumped them, before driving home to slip once more between the sheets with his sleeping wife.

The evidence against Thomas was tenuous until the police made a controversial discovery. On 27 October, Detectives Charles and Parkes went to Owen Priest's farm, and apparently popped in to say good morning, then went up to the Crewe farm and shortly afterwards found a .22 cartridge case in the flower bed, which the police were to claim had never been searched before.

The two detectives then went back to the Priest farm for a cup of tea and presumably to "prove" they had found the cartridge. According to Owen Priest, Detective Charles put on one of the Priests' daughter's hats and "danced around the room like a kid".

When examined by scientists, the extraction marks on the cartridge case were consistent with the extraction marks of a cartridge test fired by the rifle of Arthur Allan Thomas. On 11 November, Detective Inspector Bruce Hutton arrested Arthur Allan Thomas and charged him with the murders of Harvey and Jeannette Crewe.

The suggested motive was that long after both Thomas and Jeannette had married other people and despite the fact they had never had anything other than a platonic relationship, Thomas continued to be besotted by Jeannette.

In fact, this scenario was similar to the one that had taken place half a century before when a jealous Samuel Thorne had killed the returned husband of his lover. It seemed that the method of murder could also have been borrowed from the past. Thorne had shot Eyre through an open window. The prosecution in the Crewe murders contended that Thomas had done the same through the open louvre windows of the Crewe farmhouse.

What is the likelihood of two murders being committed in almost exactly the same way in the same area 50 years apart? Could the latter murderer have copied the earlier modus operandi, as it was patently successful? Or did the prosecution simply borrow from the previous incident in order to construct their own scenario?

The truth is that again there was no tangible evidence to suggest that the Crewe murders could have occurred in this way. It was wholly conjecture and should have been inadmissible as evidence.

Similarly, the evidence linking Thomas to the axle was tenuous. Inspector Hutton had felt but not seen the weight that held Harvey Crewe's body. Nor could the axle found in the river, which had no registration or serial number, be definitely linked to Thomas.

When Arthur Allan Thomas stood in the No 1 Court of the Supreme Court at Auckland on 15 February 1971 charged with the murders of Jeannette and Harvey Crewe, the key evidence against him was the cartridge case. After a trial lasting 13 days, he was found guilty of the murders and sentenced to life imprisonment.

When the appeal against his conviction was dismissed, local supporters formed the Arthur Allan Thomas Retrial Committee.

In November 1971, the committee presented a petition for a new trial signed by 24,000 people. Just before Christmas of that year, the Minister of Justice, David Thomson, announced a review was to be carried out by a retired judge of the Supreme Court, Sir George McGregor.

His report, delivered two months later, concluded there had been no miscarriage of justice. However, the report was riddled with factual errors and should not have been accepted on that basis alone. Even so, the Executive Council accepted its conclusion that there were no grounds for a new trial.

But the case was attracting so much publicity that even Robert Muldoon, the then Deputy Prime Minister, became involved. One day, Thomas' counsel, Kevin Ryan, was asked by Muldoon to meet him at the Intercontinental Hotel where he was staying in Auckland. They discussed the case in detail and Muldoon told Ryan he had even visited McGregor, who had delivered the flawed report. Muldoon said that when he rose to leave, McGregor had asked, "Which paper did you say you were from?"

On Muldoon's advice, the petition was resubmitted with amendments. In August 1972, the Governor-General referred the case back to the Court of Appeal and on 26 February 1973, in a majority decision, the Court ordered a new trial for Arthur Allan Thomas. The retrial committee and Thomas' legal representatives rejoiced.

The justice system may be just or unjust, but it is invariably slow. A trial usually takes months, sometimes as long as a year to come to court. In the case of Arthur Allan Thomas, it took just four weeks. The new trial was scheduled to start on 27 March.

The police case was already well prepared and indeed would be almost a carbon copy of the first trial. The defence had also prepared themselves well over the previous two years.

But the reason why the trial was brought forward was to give Kevin Ryan and Thomas' legal team no time to do research on the jury. In fact, Ryan only received the jury list on the Thursday before the trial which was due to start on the Monday. He frantically phoned around trying to get information on the members of the panel. That list had been deliberately held back from him.

The prosecution had had it for three weeks and police officers had investigated each prospective juror. They were able to form profiles of each and, armed with that information, the prosecution was able to select a jury with a strong bias towards the police.

The choice of Clifford Perry as judge was also unfortunate. One lawyer who knew Perry described him to me thus, "He wasn't very tall – a pigmy in height and a pigmy in intelligence. The only reason he was appointed a judge was because his brother was a bigwig in the National Party."

Ryan had defended many cases before Perry and on at least two occasions Perry's decisions had been overturned by the Court of Appeal. Perry had demonstrated animosity towards Ryan previously. They were like chalk and cheese. One slow-witted and serious, the other aggressive, sometimes to the point of brashness. For the murder case of the century, Perry was the last person Ryan wanted to have sitting before him.

Why were the police and prosecution so determined to convict Thomas?

Strangely, if Thomas and Detective Inspector Hutton had ever stood side by side in the same photograph (an extremely unlikely occurrence) you might have thought they were brothers. Hutton was a farmer before joining the police and both had uncluttered rustic faces. Both were plain, straightforward characters and both had, as journalist Warwick Roger put it, distinctive "dark eyes".

At some point in the inquiry, Hutton had obviously decided that Thomas was his man. Thomas, described by Kevin Ryan as a "straightforward country type of person", did not help by being less than vigorous in his own defence. Maybe the police interpreted his simple honesty as a front for a highly calculating mind.

Certain that he was the murderer, and knowing the evidence was insufficient, members of the police team decided that they would give the wheels of justice an extra little push. The problem with the discovery of the cartridge case in the Crewes' flower garden was that it was too simple. Evidence is usually hard won. To decide that area alone had not been searched and to go there and later find the case simply stretches credulity.

That find was just too "lucky" and the balance of probabilities is that the cartridge case was planted. To support this is the fact that the Thomas rifle was taken back by the police for "testing" immediately before the cartridge case was found.

The only reason to plant the cartridge case was to convict Thomas, and having committed such a gross act of deception the only way to justify it was to ensure he was convicted. So the matter became an obsession. Only one or two people would have known that the cartridge case was planted, but they would have infected others with their zeal for the crusade to ensure a "murderer" remained behind bars.

This was the scenario as the second "loaded dice" trial began in the Auckland Supreme Court. Much has been written in the past about the peripheral evidence in the case. Much of it, such as the last-minute evidence of the jeweller in the first trial that someone who looked like Thomas had brought in a watch similar to the one Harvey Crewe had owned, was so trivial as to be almost inadmissible. The number 8 wire that was wrapped around the bodies could have come from Thomas' farm, but in a farming community it could just as easily have come from anybody else's farm too.

In both trials, the only real "evidence" that linked Thomas directly to the murders was exhibit 350, the infamous .22 cartridge case.

The defence called on Graham Hewson to describe the search of the Crewes' property. Hewson was a close friend of Harvey Crewe. They had first met several years before in the Woodville area near Palmerston North, where Hewson farmed. Harvey Crewe had been a teenager working as a shepherd. After he had been fired by the farmer with whom he had lost his temper, Hewson had asked him to come and work for him. Crewe stayed on his farm for two years.

When he found out about Harvey Crewe's disappearance (and probable murder), Hewson drove up from Woodville with Harvey's uncle to help with the search. He managed the farm for the family until a manager could be appointed before he went back to Woodville, but returned immediately after the discovery of Jeannette's body on 16 August.

It was now virtually certain that Harvey Crewe had been murdered and Hewson was eager to help in the discovery of his friend's killer. He became an "unofficial" special constable for the police, even going so far as putting pressure on Demler when Demler was the chief suspect. The police told Hewson to tell Demler that a child specialist was teaching Rochelle to talk. According to Hewson, when he told Demler this, he went white.

Hewson was eager to help when police conducted a sieve search of the Crewe garden soon after discovering Jeannette's body. The search was meticulously carried out, with the garden divided into narrow grids using string lines so that police, on hands and knees, would not miss anything.

Hewson was excited when he found a bullet and immediately called out to the other searchers. It seemed they were as excited as he was because the policemen gathered around with smiling faces. Then they revealed they had planted it as a joke. Nothing else came to light during that search which Hewson would testify had included the area where the crucial cartridge case was later discovered.

However, several police officers refuted Hewson's evidence at the trial, claiming he had not been involved in the grid search. His character was also maligned, with allegations he had marital and financial difficulties at the time and that he had stolen Harvey Crewe's dogs (Hewson had obtained permission from the family to take them in order to look after them).

At the first trial, the Crown had made much of the fact that the bullets recovered from the Crewes' bodies were stamped with the figure 8 and that Thomas had such ammunition.

Before the second trial, the Thomas retrial committee set out to show that figure 8 ammunition was common and advertised for people to send in that type of ammunition. They drew a huge response, with ammunition flooding in from all over New Zealand.

So much ammunition arrived that the chairman of the retrial committee, Pat Vesey, had not been able to sort through it all. In April 1973, Vesey was wearily waiting to go into court to testify on behalf of Arthur Allan Thomas. He was the uncle of Vivian Thomas, who had come from England to stay with him. He had introduced her to Thomas and he felt a duty to prove his friend and in-law innocent.

As he was waiting, a strange feeling started to come over him.

"I felt a high tension, almost a lightness, as if I had no control over myself. My hands and head began to sweat. My ears began to ring and suddenly I found myself standing up and exclaiming to the people in the room, 'I've got to go home.' They all looked at me as if I was quite mad."

Vesey knocked on the door through which witnesses entered and left the court, informing Kevin Ryan's junior counsel, his twin brother, Gerald, that he was leaving. The Ryan brothers were aghast. But Vesey was a strong-willed character and he walked out of the courtroom and drove home.

"I didn't know why I was doing it," he said afterwards. "Something just compelled me."

At his house he went straight to a drawer that held all the different containers of .22 cartridges they had been sent. He reached into the drawer and without hesitation took out a box that was still wrapped. It was a fish-hook box with the price of the hooks still on it. The box had been sent by a former policeman, Jack Ritchie, who had a sports goods shop and a deep knowledge of firearms.

The box contained some envelopes and a letter. In the letter, Ritchie gave instructions for the envelopes to be opened in a particular order. Vesey opened the envelopes in turn, using pliers to pull the bullets from the cartridge cases.

As he did so, Vesey saw a clear pattern developing. "According to the type of case from which it came, it was possible to predict with 100 per cent accuracy whether a bullet would carry the figure 8. As Ritchie said, it might well be that exhibit 350, the 'crucial' evidence, was of a type that did not carry figure 8 bullets."

Vesey immediately returned to the court to make his discovery known to the Thomas legal team. If this had been a Hollywood movie, this was the point where the case would have been won, but in my opinion it was here that the defence probably made their second fundamental error.

The first was when they agreed to rush to trial, no doubt in the belief that justice was now on their side and the quicker Thomas was released the better.

The second error the defence made was not calling Jack Ritchie as the principal witness to testify about the cartridge case and the number 8 bullet. He was the one who had first identified the problem, he was obviously knowledgeable about firearms, and his testimony would have carried great weight because he was also a former policeman.

When the cartridge case was found, the defence called analyst Dr Jim Sprott to give evidence that the number 8 bullet could not have come from the cartridge case found in the Crewe flower bed. He devised diagrams to attempt to make the point clear to the jury. The prosecution quickly found their own experts, who gave the opposite point of view. The jury ended up being confused on this point but not enough to reject the prosecution's argument about the cartridge case.

At this point, the trial had degenerated into a trial by experts, which is often similar to the children's trick of claiming "my brother is bigger than your brother".

There were two other matters of note in the second trial. One was that Thomas chose to take the stand in his own defence and suffer the cross-examination of the prosecutor David Morris. He collapsed at the end of it, which was further proof of his innocence to his supporters and further proof of his guilt to his accusers. One assistant registrar was heard to loudly describe Thomas' collapse in open court as a "Hollywood".

But as fascinating as the murder was, what really gripped the nation was Rochelle Crewe being abandoned in the murder house alone for several days. But was she alone for all that time? Many saw it as the key to the whole case. Again the matter was fudged somewhat by experts on both sides disagreeing about whether she had been fed.

More tangible evidence were the nappies. She had been changed until the supply had been used up. Soiled nappies had been discarded rather than put away.

When Demler and Priest entered the house on 22 June, they did not immediately notice she had not been fed for several days. In fact, they left her to go outside and look for the bodies.

There was other evidence that someone had been at the property. On the morning of Friday 19 June, a local farmer, Frederick Hoskins, heard the Crewe farm cows bellowing to be fed. As the bellowing later stopped, it can be assumed someone fed them.

That day, a farmhand, Bruce Roddick, who was working at a farm opposite, saw a European woman dressed in slacks standing near the Crewe farmhouse. He later attended an identification parade which included Vivian Thomas. He had already told the police she was not the woman he saw and did not pick her out.

That evening, at about 7.30 pm, sparks were seen coming out of the Crewe farmhouse chimney, presumably as the murderer burnt the rug.

On the Saturday, Queenie McConachie was driving by the property. At the time she was pregnant and so had a heightened interest in children. She saw a child at the front gate a few yards from the road who was wearing long blue trousers with a bib front (similar to the clothes Rochelle was wearing when found). McConachie watched her toddle up the path.

On Monday 22 June, a deliveryman noticed that curtains which had been closed on the Thursday morning were now open.

When Graham Hewson arrived straight after the discovery of the tragedy, he said the Crewes' dogs were as "fat as seals". They had obviously been fed.

A police photograph of Rochelle a few days after she was discovered alone in the house shows her looking chubby and well. It seemed she had also been fed. If only she could have spoken. She must have seen the murderer.

At the trial, the nails were hammered into Arthur Allan Thomas' coffin a second time by a devastating final address by David Morris, which mixed facts and supposition in a seamless blend and encouraged the jury to fill in the gaps in the way he wanted.

He was much criticised afterwards for his statement, "We also know that a long hearth mat and cushion were at some stage burned by the murderer, and also that the room was heavily bloodstained. Whether the burning of these items was like the use of two saucepans with a view to concealing the blood, or whether it was done to conceal other marks traceable to the killer or his treatment of Jeannette we do not know."

When he heard these words, "or his treatment of Jeannette", Kevin Ryan, like members of the jury, took them to mean semen, which implied a sexual attack on Jeannette. Ryan was stunned and in those few seconds considered objecting, but did not because he didn't want to draw any attention to Morris' implied assertion.

The truth was that it was almost certain that no sexual attack had been made on Jeannette. When her body was found, she was fully clothed. Her pantyhose were intact. There were no rips or tears of her clothes, in fact there was no evidence at all to imply sexual assault. Yet the wording used by Morris cunningly tied the murders into the prosecution theme that sex was the motive for Thomas to have committed the crime.

Kevin Ryan's final address was made on the Friday and Justice Perry gave his summing-up and the jury retired to consider their verdict early the next week. They quickly decided that Thomas was guilty, but lingered in the jury room a while so that no one thought they had rushed to a verdict. While they were twiddling their thumbs, someone suggested they while away the time with a vote on whether they thought the cartridge case had been planted.

When they came out, the court was so packed with friends and relatives of Thomas that many were forced to wait outside because there was not enough room. When Thomas was found guilty, the crowd inside let out a deep animal sound of pain and started chanting, "He's not guilty". Outside, the supporters heard the chant and started celebrating because they thought he had been acquitted.

When they discovered the truth, smiles turned to anguished faces and tears. The moment is captured in a photograph of Arthur Allan Thomas' brother Ray gripping the hand of his wife, Robyn. The look of shock and anguish on his face is far deeper than any physical pain could be. It is intense. It is absolute.

Pandemonium broke out in the courthouse as Arthur Allan Thomas was taken back to Paremoremo Maximum Security Prison, photographers catching the look of utter despair and defeat on his face as he was driven away in a police car.

Many felt that justice had not been done but, instead of weakening, the resolve of Thomas' supporters grew even stronger.

Pat Booth, of the "Auckland Star", wrote a series of investigative articles. British author David Yallop wrote a book about the saga, "Beyond Reasonable Doubt", which was made into a film.

Another petition was made to the Governor-General,

who referred it to a five-member bench of the Court of Appeal. When that was unsuccessful, the case was taken to the Privy Council in England, which decided it had no jurisdiction over the matter.

By 1978, Rob Muldoon had become Prime Minister and he assigned an Auckland QC, Robert Adams-Smith, to make an independent report. His report was published in December 1979. It concluded that the prosecution case had not been proved "beyond reasonable doubt" and recommended that Thomas be pardoned. After more than nine years in prison, Arthur Allan Thomas was finally set free.

Though that seemed to be the end of the tale, it wasn't. In June 1980, a Royal Commission of Inquiry was set up to investigate. During that time, Kevin Ryan was searching through police files when he found the jobsheet of a detective sergeant from Otahuhu called Toothill.

On the jobsheet, Toothill had recorded going to the Crewe farm during August 1970 and seeing Hewson helping the police to search the Crewes' garden. Hewson was vindicated.

Evidence was also uncovered which revealed that, a few days before the discovery of the cartridge case, Detective Sergeant Len Johnston had collected Thomas' rifle and also some ammunition from his farm. The ammunition was only given to the exhibits officer after the cartridge case had been discovered.

After hearing evidence from nearly 150 witnesses and receiving written statements from another 50, the commission's report was presented in November 1980. It was highly critical of the police and found that the cartridge case had been planted by Detective Inspector Hutton and Detective Sergeant Len Johnston (who had died two years earlier).

Hutton vigorously denied the allegation and in 1982 the Police Association tried to have the findings overturned by the Court of Appeal but the court ruled they must stand.

At first jubilation...

News Media Auckland

...then agonising despair.

News Media Auckland

Arthur Allan Thomas was awarded compensation of $950,000. He and Vivian Thomas had been divorced in 1976 while he was still in prison.

On 17 June 1970, between 8.15 and 8.45 pm, Julie Priest was on her farm about half a mile away when she heard three shots coming from the Crewe farm. So who did it? Who walked into the Crewe farmhouse that night and orphaned 18-month-old Rochelle?

As far as the police are concerned, a man has been twice convicted of the Crewe murders and the case is closed. As far as the public are concerned, that man was pardoned and is innocent.

I have laid out the material facts. They seem to point the finger at one person. I leave you to be the judge and jury as to who stole up to a lonely farmhouse on a windy night and murdered Harvey and Jeannette Crewe.

5. Mona Blades

Death in an Orange Datsun

The Saturday of Queen's Birthday weekend, 31 May 1975, dawned cloudy and mild. In Hamilton, a cheerful teenage girl decided to visit her parents in Hastings. Her name was Mona Blades.

Mona was a bit of a tomboy. She stood just 1.63m tall and was best described as a well-built girl. She had blue eyes, a fair complexion and shoulder-length, honey-blonde hair. Friends said she had a sparkling smile and a loving nature, especially towards children. She enjoyed horse riding and her main hobbies were acquiring stamps and matchboxes, of which she had quite a collection.

Mona was an experienced hitchhiker. Before she moved in to live with her sister Lillian, she had often hitchhiked to Hamilton to visit her. When Lillian's first child, Angela, was born, Mona had hitchhiked for a surprise visit and presented the newborn baby with a pair of booties.

Now that she was living in Hamilton, Mona often hitchhiked to visit her parents in Hastings. She had hitchhiked along the Napier-Taupo highway at least two dozen times in the past year. She always made sure to write home first to tell them she was coming.

This time she didn't. Instead she wrote to a friend in Hastings to say she would be in town that weekend. She didn't tell her parents because she wanted to surprise her nephew Quentin, who was celebrating his first birthday.

Mona left home at 7 am that morning. She was dressed in a black duffel coat, long green trousers, a fawn jersey and a green football jersey. She was carrying a brown canvas pack inside which were the presents for her nephew. Her brother-in-law Tom drove her south of the city and dropped her off at Cambridge Road.

She told him she would see him on Monday. She had to be back by then as on the Tuesday she was due to start a new job at a dairy in the Hamilton suburb of Dinsdale. She was in high spirits as she stood in light rain waving him goodbye. That was the last time Tom would see her.

As the long weekend drew to a close, Lillian started to become concerned that Mona had not arrived home. She did not want her to be late for her new job. She phoned her mother to find out what was keeping her and was stunned to be told Mona had never arrived.

At first the police treated Mona as a missing person and believed she would turn up. But Lillian knew Mona wouldn't have just taken off. Jobs were hard to find and it had taken her a month to find the dairy job. Besides, she wasn't the type of person to just disappear.

When the police visited Lillian's house to get Mona's fingerprints, Lillian knew then her disappearance was being treated as a murder inquiry.

By coincidence, the man leading the search for Mona was the family's next-door neighbour Detective Inspector Phil Berryman. As the days dragged on with no trace of Mona, he would pop by for coffee to update them on the progress of the investigation.

Police attempts to track Mona's movements were at first distracted by red herrings. Some of the earliest reported sightings of Mona were discovered to have been those of another woman hitchhiking in the Taupo region on Queen's Birthday weekend. When this other hitchhiker contacted police to tell them that she wore a green jersey similar to the one Mona had been wearing, a note of her movements was taken and discounted from the inquiry.

An Australian hitchhiker touring New Zealand, Julie Blade, also initially confused police. She had made ferry bookings to the South Island at the time.

Gradually, a clearer picture of Mona's movements on that day began to emerge. It hadn't taken Mona long to thumb a lift. A Hamilton man picked her up and dropped her off at the intersection of State Highway 1 and State Highway 5 at Tirau.

South of Tirau, at the Rotorua turnoff junction, Mona was picked up by an Auckland woman who was driving a turquoise Volkswagen. The two women chatted happily on the journey. Mona Blades told the woman she was going home and told her about the presents she had bought for her nephew.

The woman dropped Mona off in Taupo at about 10.10 am. The rain was falling harder now and many people recalled her walking along Lake Terrace conspicuously dressed in her long green trousers and black duffel coat. She called in at the Taupo information centre where she cheerfully told staff she was going to Hastings to pay her parents a surprise visit.

She then made her way to the Napier highway turnoff. At some time between 10 and 11 am, a truck driver saw a young woman fitting Mona's description get into an orange Datsun 1200 station wagon. The truck driver got a glimpse of the man behind the wheel. He estimated that he was 40 to 50 years old with a fattish face, prominent forehead and receding hairline.

The station wagon set off down the highway, with Mona sitting in the front seat next to the balding man. Forty kilometres later, the Datsun suddenly turned off down Matea Rd, a metalled side-road that served a Lands and Survey farm block. The rain was now turning to mist and as it enveloped Matea Rd, the truck driver saw the station wagon came to a halt about 200 metres from the highway.

The truck driver drove on towards Napier.

Soon afterwards, at about 11 am, a local fencing contractor who lived on Matea Rd was driving along the main road. He glanced across and saw two people in a Datsun. One was a middle-aged man and the other was a young woman wearing a black duffel coat. She was sitting in the back of the car.

When the fencing contractor drove back a few minutes later, the Datsun was still parked in the same place, but this time he saw only the middle-aged man sitting in the car.

The orange Datsun station wagon was next sighted by a farmer being driven down Matea Rd.

A person who had been visiting a farmhouse about two kilometres down Matea Rd also saw the Datsun travelling slowly down the road in a direction away from the Napier-Taupo highway. This witness said the driver had glasses, a receding hairline and a prominent forehead.

The search for Mona concentrated on the Matea Rd area. The road runs through a 16,000ha Lands and Survey farming development block which sits at more than 670m above sea level, south of Rangitaiki and about 45 kilometres south-west of Taupo. It is mainly open farmland with culverts, scrub, and water-scoured pumice gulches. Tussock scrub and low brush outcrops extend for kilometres. It is the type of forbidding countryside

News Media Auckland

The forbidding Matea Road where Mona Blades was last seen.

where a body could easily be hidden.

The search for Mona went on in falling snow as policemen fanned out into the Kaingaroa State Forest and continued along the Mohaka River, eight miles south of Tarawera on the Napier-Taupo highway. A swamp was also searched, though technically it is not possible to really search a swamp.

About 8 kilometres down Matea Road was a spoil site where a great mound of earth had been dumped. A bulldozer was brought in to move the earthworks in case her body was buried there.

Two Thames deerstalkers came forward to say they had seen an orange Datsun station wagon parked in scrub off the Taupo-Napier road. They went with police to pinpoint the exact location. Following this, policemen equipped with ropes and climbing equipment explored caves and holes in the hills surrounding the Runanga Gorge.

RNZAF helicopters armed with electronic scanning devices swept the area to try to discover where the body might be buried. It was the first time the infrared heat sensors, which were sensitive enough to find the body of a dead rabbit, had been used in New Zealand. Some hot spots were discovered, but digging them up was delayed by bad weather. When the weather cleared, no body was found.

Areas where the Datsun had been seen were thoroughly searched. Grass where it had been parked was scythed and the area grid-searched. An army field kitchen had to be brought in to feed all the searchers.

The search was scaled down, but gained new impetus when a burn-off on a Lands and Survey block, Wahakatau, got out of control. The Forest Service had planned to burn only 1600ha of crushed scrub for the Lands and Survey Department but the fires had jumped firebreaks and spread over a further 1200ha set aside for burning the following year. The cleared land was searched, but again there was no sign of Mona Blades.

Without the body being found, the police search now focussed on the Datsun. Any sighting of an orange Datsun station wagon on the Taupo-Napier road on 31 May was followed up.

A truck driver reported that the owner of the orange Datsun station wagon might have talked to two youths whose car had broken down by the side of the road. The sighting was about 45 kilometres from Taupo near Rangitaiki when he was travelling towards Napier just after midday. On the side of the road he had seen a Mark III Zephyr, which was painted in grey primer. The car had a puncture and was jacked up. On the opposite side of the road, two men stood with a wheel from the car, obviously trying to hitchhike back into Taupo to get it fixed. Both were Maori.

From the other direction, the truck driver saw the orange Datsun approaching from Napier. It slowed down and it seemed to the truck driver that the driver of the Datsun could have spoken to the two youths and possibly given them a lift.

The driver said he later saw the same car in either Waipukurau or Dannevirke about 6 pm that day. Inside were four people, two of them Maori youths and another could have been a fair-haired girl.

A few days later, a man came forward who had talked to the occupants of the Zephyr (he was not the one driving an orange station wagon). He said he got the impression from the young men that the car had come from Whangarei.

This came to nothing, but another lead was more promising. A 21-year-old Australian hitchhiker from Sydney who was on a working holiday in New Zealand told police she had been given a lift from Taupo to Wairakei in an orange Datsun station wagon on Queen's Birthday weekend.

The woman, who at the time was living in Auckland, described the driver as having a fat face, receding light brown hair and wearing sports clothes. She estimated that he was aged between 30 and 40.

Clothes had been scattered around in the back of his two-door vehicle. She also noticed there was a pair of sunglasses with blue lenses on the seat.

The woman felt uneasy with the driver. She had talked to him out of politeness and also to try to put herself at ease. He gave her the impression from what he said that he had spent the weekend in the Taupo area. Finally, unnerved by his odd manner, she asked him to let her out. He did and she stood by the side of the road and watched him drive away with a feeling of relief.

The police tried to track down a middle-aged couple who gave the woman a lift soon after the Datsun had dropped her off. They were hoping that the couple had seen the Datsun and had recalled the registration plate number, but this lead also came to nothing.

Based on the various sightings, the police issued identikit pictures to the news media.

There was another report that a girl hitchhiker in the South Island had been attacked by a man driving an orange station wagon. This was investigated and found to be unrelated.

Any Datsun that was proved to be on the road that day underwent rigorous forensic testing. A Datsun from

Rotorua was eliminated from the inquiry. Hopes were raised when another Datsun was investigated that had blood on a panel but tests showed that the blood had come from an animal.

During the course of the inquiry, the police managed to track down all of the more than 300 Datsun station wagons that had been painted orange when sold new and eliminated them from their inquiries.

There were many other Datsun station wagons that had first been registered in a different colour, but which had since been painted orange. They were more difficult to track down though the investigation was aided by the fact that just three years before the Post Office had made provision for the inclusion of the colour of cars on motor registration forms. Car painters and car dealers who had handled orange Datsun station wagons since 31 May were asked to contact the police.

For a short time in New Zealand, driving an orange Datsun station wagon, especially if you were a middle-aged man with a receding hairline, invited immediate suspicion.

"I can't take the car on the road without being pointed at," said one Datsun owner, who was balding, wore glasses and bore a strong resemblance to the identikit picture of the man the police were seeking.

"You couldn't imagine the hell I've been through," he said. "To put a stop to the gossip, I've started going to work on the bus." He no longer used the car but left it locked away in the garage, well out of sight.

Others who had had enough of pointing fingers and accusing glances decided to get their cars repainted. Of course, as soon as they were out of earshot, the garage owner or mechanic would phone the police, so that the poor driver would end up being investigated further.

Detective Inspector Berryman, who was in charge of the investigation, admitted at the time that Datsun station wagon owners wanted "to be able to walk down the street and hold their heads up again". He announced in the news

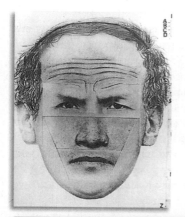

News Media Auckland

Identikit pictures of the chief suspects
circulated by police.

News Media Auckland

The police investigation team with an orange
Datsun station wagon.

media that the police had issued special letters to owners whose orange Datsuns had been eliminated from the inquiry.

In July, there was a sensational new lead when a letter was received from a Gisborne schoolgirl who gave no name and no address. The letter, which was written in small, neat handwriting, said: "I was on the road the same morning as Miss Blades. I was also picked up by an orange Datsun station wagon, but I said I changed my mind and was going to Rotorua. He was too fresh and said he was going to Napier. I later was given a ride by an elderly couple and we passed the same station wagon parked on the roadside on the Napier road.

"It was the same car that I had been in but there was nobody in it. I mentioned this to the people in the car. They were going to see their daughter and her family in Hastings.

"My parents wouldn't let me come forward before because they didn't wish to become involved and I thought you would have caught the man by now.

"I hope this will help you but I cannot give you my name for my parents will not understand."

Appeals were made for the writer of the letter to come forward. It was possible the police could have located her if they had taken her fingerprints from the letter. Then they could have sent a copy of the letter to every schoolteacher in Gisborne and asked them to identify the handwriting. Those girls whose handwriting was nominated to be similar to that of the letter by their teachers could have then been fingerprinted to definitely identify the writer.

But, even if located, it is uncertain what further help the girl could have given other than a more detailed description of the driver – if her letter was indeed genuine.

In July 1980, well-known British psychic Doris Stokes came to New Zealand. Stokes was a working-class, middle-aged woman who was quite ordinary to look at and who conducted herself in a very ordinary grandmotherly manner that made her seem instantly believable.

There seems little doubt that she had genuine psychic abilities, though at one time she had confessed to some fraudulent activity. She operated by hearing the voices of dead spirits, who stood near her and spoke to her. She admitted that at one time, when the voices were not coming through, and under pressure from relatives desperate to talk to their loved ones, she had invented the responses from the dead. But she said she had done this on only one occasion.

Stokes appeared on television with both Detective Inspector Berryman and Mona's sister Lillian. She told Lillian that her father and brothers both had the same name and that her brother went by a nickname – information that she was unlikely to have come across by accident. She told Lillian how her grandmother died, something that Lillian had not even been aware of.

Berryman said he had found Stokes to be "a sincere, well-meaning woman" who had told him things she could not have known otherwise.

She told him a name inscribed on the back of a wristwatch which was found near the Waipunga Falls, off the Taupo-Napier highway, which was correct. Stokes also gave him information about a letter Mona had written a few days before her disappearance but which she had never posted. Stokes accurately said that the letter was addressed to a friend called Susan. She also told him a registration plate number which coincided with the one given to the police by another witness.

Though Stokes could have probably got the information of the location from the newspapers, Berryman was impressed that she chose an area that was accurate within about ten kilometres.

But the crucial question was, did she know where the body was buried?

Stokes said she believed it was in the vicinity of the waterfall where there was a short, dead-end road. This fitted the description of the Waipunga Falls, which had already undergone an intensive search.

The police decided to search the area again but because of the rugged and dangerous terrain, which was exacerbated by the winter conditions with snow on the ground and swollen rivers, and because of the five years that had elapsed, they would leave the search until the weather cleared.

When the police did search the area, they found no sign of a body. Later bones were found beside the road, but they turned out to be the bones of a sheep.

Stokes wrote many books about her experiences and in her fifth book, "Whispering Voices", she told a tale that seemed to parallel the Mona Blades mystery. She said she was in New Zealand when a girl murder victim contacted her from the spirit world. The spirit described the landscape she remembered in her last moments. "It was winter time and the whole area was covered in snow," Stokes wrote in the book.

Unfortunately, Stokes got the name of the girl wrong. She recalled her as Susan, rather than Mona, probably confusing Mona with the friend that Mona had written the letter to which she never sent. She also wrote in the book, "Later, when the snows cleared, the police went back and searched the place and sure enough they found the body. I had pinpointed it within 500 yards."

Stokes made vague references to the murderer, but nothing concrete. So who was he?

The police had not revealed they were searching for an orange Datsun station wagon immediately. It was on 12 June 1975 that they made that announcement. On that day, a former inmate of a mental institution, 26-year-old John Walton Freeman, left work at midday claiming he was sick. The next day was Friday 13th – Black Friday – and Freeman had already worked out how he was going to celebrate it.

Freeman has been described as "a man who lived inside

himself". He came out from England in 1964 with his parents, who settled in the Waikato area. He was intelligent and attended Te Awamutu College followed by Otago University, where he enrolled for a science degree, but dropped out after just four weeks because of "personality problems".

After that, Freeman became something of a drifter.

In 1969, in Te Awamutu, Freeman was crossing a level crossing on his motorbike when he was struck by a goods train. He recovered from serious physical injuries, but it appears the accident worsened his already fragile mental state. One person who knew him at the time said, "He was never the same again."

A curious incident occurred at this time which might have had a bearing on Mona Blades' disappearance.

Freeman took a local woman out in his van. At one stage, instead of driving her home, Freeman took her to nearby Mt Pirongia. They argued along the way and the woman says that Freeman "went mad with rage and his face went white". When they arrived at the mountain, the woman climbed out of the van and tried to run away but Freeman grabbed her and slammed her against the side of the vehicle.

The next thing she remembered was waking up lying across the front seat of the van outside her home. Her blouse was torn, her stockings were missing and she was bleeding from the vagina. The next day, distinct fingermark bruising appeared around her neck.

The woman's parents, Freeman's parents, a doctor and a local policeman were all involved in a talk about the incident but it was decided no formal complaint would be made to the police.

Freeman left the town shortly afterwards for holiday work. When he returned, the local policeman spoke to him about his boxer dog. Though the dog was generally well behaved, it had got into the habit of defecating on the policeman's lawn. The policeman had merely wanted

Freeman to discourage the dog from doing so. The policeman was shocked when Freeman took the dog to the local vet and had it put down.

For the next few months, Freeman lead a nomadic life of crime, stealing, among other things, a yacht. He was arrested when he ran the yacht aground at Whakatane. A policeman arrived who did not know the yacht was stolen and tried to help him refloat it. Freeman responded by pulling a gun on him.

Freeman was arrested and in April 1969 he was brought before the magistrate's court on charges of possessing an illegal firearm, stealing a horse, a motor car and a yacht. He was remanded to Tokanui Mental Hospital, but escaped a month later. He was recaptured, but released back into the community a week later.

After his release, he drifted around the country taking various jobs in various areas. He worked for Westfield Freezing Works (Auckland), Abel's Margarine Factory (Auckland), the New Zealand Army (Hamilton), the Auckland Hospital Board, Hellabys (Auckland), Watties (Napier), Downer Tunnelling (Tokaanu), the Wellington Hospital Board and finally Pakuranga Steel and Tube Ltd.

For this last job, he boarded in a tiny, damp "hut" at the rear of a boarding house in Moa Rd, Otahuhu. At the boarding house, he spent all his time alone, never sitting in the kitchen to join in general conversation or going with the other young men to a hotel for a drink.

It was the same story at work. Freeman would sit alone at the staff cafeteria; at lunch times he would go for a ride on his red Honda 50cc motorbike.

The only time he ever joined in the general conversation was when one man was reading a magazine about vehicles used by the German Army's Afrika Corps during the Second World War. Freeman immediately began to tell the man the full history of the vehicles, including the armaments and the engines. When police later inspected Freeman's one-room hut, they found piles of military magazines and books.

On 12 June 1975, the day he left work early, Freeman did not sleep the night in his hut. Instead he booked into a motel in Epsom. The next morning, he rose early and made his way to St Cuthbert's College, Epsom. Either there or at some point earlier, he had dressed himself in full army assault kit, including balaclava, a bandolier over his shoulder and a bayonet thrust into his belt. He was armed with a .303 Lee Enfield rifle and 50 rounds of ammunition.

He took up position hidden in the basement of a school outbuilding and waited.

Slowly the schoolgirls began to arrive, laughing and playing, before the school day started.

A military ambush is the only way to describe it. Freeman was less than 10 metres away from his young targets. He loosed off three or four shots in quick succession. One struck a concrete path just a few metres in front of him. But his aim was not accurate because he had sawn 22cm off the end of the barrel. Other bullets flew harmlessly into the air.

But one struck a 13-year-old schoolgirl, Rosemary Smith, in the pelvis. The girl survived, but seeing her hit, perhaps Freeman considered he had achieved what he had set out to do. Or he had realised what he had actually done and was struck by remorse.

Either way he turned the gun on himself, pushing the muzzle into his mouth and squeezing the trigger at point-blank range. It is not easy to commit suicide with a full-length rifle and it is possible that Freeman always intended killing himself when his spree was over and that was why he had sawn off the end of the barrel.

The girl survived and recovered.

The police discovered another 80 rounds of ammunition with his body. Later, they also found a cache of guns and ammunition hidden in a field near his work. If Freeman had fully carried out his plan, the carnage would have been gruesome.

Freeman was cremated at Waikumete Cemetery with

only one person in attendance – a policeman. At the time, his ashes were held pending directions from his parents who had long since returned to Britain. There is no record whether they ever wanted or received them.

What made Freeman of interest to the police on the Mona Blades inquiry was that, on 30 May, Freeman had hired a 1200cc orange Datsun station wagon. The car that he had hired from Andrew and Andrew Rentals Ltd had the registration number GZ5630.

In the past he had been a regular customer of the firm and this time told staff that he was going to use the car to drive around Auckland. Staff later told police that they thought Freeman looked like the identikit picture when it was released, but they considered the station wagon was brown orange, not orange, which was why they did not connect the car and Freeman with the crime.

When Freeman had returned the car to the rental firm, it had been filthy and required five pints of oil. There was oil all over the engine and on the windscreen, and the exterior was covered in a white, pumice clay.

There was more clay inside on both the rear and front floor. The car was so dirty on the inside that it was said it looked like he had been living in it. The cleaner also said the car had a strange smell and there was a sticky substance on the rear seat which could have been semen.

Though Freeman had hired cars from Andrew and Andrew on seven previous occasions, the manager was so disgusted by the state of the car he told Freeman he would not be allowed to hire any more. The rental company then thoroughly cleaned the car. All the loose material was removed and the car was steam-cleaned. Any evidence showing Mona had been in the car was likely to have been washed away.

The speedometer was not in a sealed unit. It was possible for someone who knew what they were doing to unscrew it and wind back the clock. That's what the manager suspected Freeman had done. In the past when Freeman had hired cars, the average speedometer reading was 240km. This time Freeman had travelled only 187km.

When the police discovered the link with Freeman, the rental company Datsun was subjected to a minute examination by DSIR scientists who took samples away for analysis. But nothing was discovered to link him to the crime.

After Freeman's death, the police took Mona's sister back to Freeman's hut to look through his clothes and see if any belonged to her sister. She did not recognise any.

Even if Freeman had not died, it appeared that the police would have had trouble pursuing a case against him because he had an alibi. Two men who stayed at the Otahuhu boarding house claimed to have seen Freeman and his hired station wagon outside the boarding house between 9 am and 9.45 am on 31 May, the Saturday of Queen's Birthday weekend. The witnesses said they were positive of the date because they borrowed special equipment from their workplace that weekend and it was the only weekend they did so.

As they worked on their car, they noticed Freeman loading blankets and pillows into the orange Datsun station wagon that was parked opposite the shed where he lived.

If that were the case, it would have been impossible for Freeman to have driven to the outskirts of Taupo by 10 am to pick up Mona.

However, the two men were interviewed by Hamilton-based detectives working directly on the Mona Blades inquiry some seven weeks after the event and no check was made at their workplace to verify which weekend they had borrowed the equipment.

Also, the detectives questioned only two of the occupants of the house. When an Auckland-based detective, Bert Merritt, went to the house just three weeks after Mona disappeared, he talked to other occupants of the house, who had an entirely different story to tell.

They recalled playing softball in the street that morning

and said that Freeman's rental car, which they had not seen parked on the premises the night before, could not have been there or it would have interfered with their game. Merritt had no doubt that the softball players were telling the truth. "I can recall it quite clearly. I had interviews with five or six of them."

But when he returned to the office with the jobsheets recording the interviews, he was told they were not needed. The Hamilton-based team were apparently uninterested because they were investigating a Rotorua man at the time, although this line of inquiry turned out to be fruitless.

There has not been a funeral or a memorial service for Mona. Her family did not want one without a body and to date her body has not been found. But her niece Angela, who bears a strong resemblance to Mona and to whom Mona gave the baby boots so long ago, still feels the presence of her aunty around her. When she goes to bed at night, she rests her head on a pillow that belonged to Mona.

So who was the driver of the orange Datsun? Was it John Freeman? He was a man of unsound mind who had already committed a recorded attack on a woman when he hired the orange Datsun station wagon on 30 May. For months, he had been planning to make an assault on a girls' school, probably realising that he would be captured. Did he set out for Te Awamutu to say goodbye to old friends before he carried out the ambush? Then instead did he detour to Taupo and pick up Mona, who was standing hitchhiking in the rain?

One theory is that, by accident or design, Freeman parked the car tight against the bank of Matea Rd making it impossible for Mona, sitting in the passenger seat, to open her door to get out. Freeman made sexual advances on Mona, who fought back.

She was something of a tomboy and relatively strong for a woman. In the struggle, she had fought her way into the back of the Datsun, but there was no escape from there because the vehicle had only two doors. At that point, it is probable that Freeman sexually violated her and killed her.

Then Freeman drove further along Matea Rd, which was 15 kilometres long and linked up with forestry roads that went right through the Kaingaroa Forest. One road went out to Iwitahi on the Taupo-Napier highway, and the other went to Murupara.

But first he drove deep into the bush and buried Mona's body somewhere where she would not be found. That might explain the dirt on the outside of the vehicle and why it needed so much oil – because he had overworked the engine driving across scrub country.

The dirt inside the car might have come from Freeman's shoes where it had stuck to him as he dug Mona's grave before rain washed away his tyre tracks.

On that Saturday night, at about 9.30 pm, a man called at the service station at Pokeno and bought a pint of oil as well as having his engine wiped clean of oil. The attendant said the man, who was alone and travelling north, resembled Freeman.

It is true that the man seen in the Datsun was described as middle-aged. Freeman was, in fact, younger but he was balding and most people saw him through rain.

Some of the descriptions said the man wore glasses. Sunglasses were found on Freeman after he died which were similar to the ones the man in the identikit picture was supposed to be wearing. They were a type which darken as more light shines on them.

The clock on the Datsun seemed to show the Datsun had only travelled 187km and therefore Freeman could never have gone to Matea Rd. But on either the Saturday or the Monday of Queen's Birthday weekend, a bus driver, who had previously been a traffic officer, recalled an orange Datsun station wagon coming up fast behind him then cutting in front of him near the Hinehopu tea rooms, near Rotorua. The driver said the car's registration number was either GZ5630 (the car hired by Freeman) or GZ5632 (a Holden Belmont).

"I am reasonably sure the number was one of these," he told police.

Did Freeman wind back the clock out of habit or after he had committed the crime? Was he the murderer of the cheerful tomboy Mona Blades?

The Ring

Another hot summer's day mellowed into a warm evening on Thursday 29 January 1976. Tracey Ann Patient was an attractive 13-year-old enjoying the end of the summer holidays at an age when childhood begins to flower into womanhood. Those early teenage years can be an awkward and in many ways a dangerous age for anybody, and that turned out to be the case for Tracey Patient.

At about 8.40 am on 30 January 1976, a young man was taking his dog for a walk in the bush around Scenic Drive near the Waitakere reservoir, West Auckland. The spot was near a lay-by off the road, popular as a "lovers' lane".

The dog became excited by something in the bush. It began to bark furiously, pulling at its leash. The young man followed the dog into the scrub and straight to the body of a young girl lying in the bushes. It was Tracey Patient.

The police were called immediately. Tracey's body was dressed in a collarless red and black cardigan which was zipped up at the front. It had large black bands patterned on the shoulders, the arms and the elbows. Underneath, she wore a blue skivvy and blue corduroy slacks. The fastener of her slacks was undone and the zip had been undone about three-quarters of the way. Her underpants had been rolled down to just below her buttocks.

Lying nearby were the leather jandals she had been wearing, one of which had a broken strap.

The most horrifying feature of her dead body was that a pair of pantyhose was tied around her neck in a loose knot, and a stick about six inches long had been inserted into the knot. As the murderer had twisted the stick, Tracey's long blonde hair had been caught up in the knot. The foot section of a pair of pantyhose was lying close by.

Tracey had been reported missing the night before. That morning, a policeman knocked on the door of the Patient house and asked Tracey's father, John, to accompany him to the station.

There John immediately felt uneasy when he saw the pained expression on the desk sergeant's face. He was told that the body of a young girl had been found in the Waitakere Ranges. "It might not be your daughter, sir," the desk sergeant told him, but John knew. He had to go to the toilet, where he dry-retched.

He did not go out to the spot where his daughter had been found. A neighbour who was a policeman went instead and formally identified the body. Then he had to come back to the police station and break the news to John Patient. There cannot be a more difficult task in life than to tell a parent their child is dead.

Tracey was a 13-year-old who loved sports and music. She was learning to play the guitar and was in the school

Police investigate the spot on Scenic Drive where the body of Tracey Patient was found.

News Media Auckland

choir. She was also mad about horses and had planned to buy a horse when she had enough money.

One thing that did set Tracey apart was that she was probably the prettiest girl in her class, with long blonde hair that she sometimes wore in plaits. She was five feet two inches tall with a slim figure. She had attractive hazel eyes, slightly rounded cheeks and a small mouth with slightly pursed lips.

Tracey had lived in Delwood Ave, Henderson, with her parents and her two sisters, 15-year-old Debbie and 10-year-old Denise. The family had originally come from the East End of London. In 1973, John and June Patient uprooted their family and emigrated to New Zealand, partly because they wanted a change but also, ironically, because they thought New Zealand and its outdoor lifestyle would be a better place to bring up their young daughters.

They chose to settle in Henderson in the west of Auckland. At first, they did not have much money and the family lived in a caravan while John, who was a roofer, rebuilt an old house into one suitable for the family to live in.

The Thursday night that Tracey disappeared, she was supposed to have gone to a Doobie Brothers concert at Western Springs, but because of a mix-up over the tickets she was at home instead. During that day, she went to see a film in Henderson with her mother and her sisters. Afterwards, they ate tea and cakes in a restaurant before catching the train home.

During the school term, the girls never went out on Thursday night because it was a homework night. But this was holiday time and there was no homework to hand in the following day. It was Tracey's sister Debbie who went to the concert at Western Springs and since Tracey had missed out on that, her mother didn't refuse her when Tracey asked to go and visit her girlfriend Sarah (a pseudonym). The only condition was that she be back in bed by 10 pm.

The last memory June Patient has of Tracey is of her running down the front path. It was 7.30 pm.

At 9 pm, June received a phone call from Tracey to say she was on her way home. That was the last time she heard her voice.

According to an interview with the parents years later, they began to be concerned when Tracey did not arrive home by 10 o'clock. Then John called the police and all the local hospitals and when he had no luck with that he drove his car around the area looking for his daughter.

According to statements taken at the time, though the parents felt some concern that Tracey had not returned, after watching television they went to bed at 11 pm. When Tracey had not returned by midnight, Mrs Patient got out of bed and phoned Sarah's parents. She was horrified to discover that Tracey and Sarah had gone out together at 9.30 pm, but they had parted soon after.

As soon as she had hung up from that call, Mrs Patient called Henderson Police Station. The police immediately started a search for Tracey. They also went to the house of her boyfriend to see if she had gone there. While the police were searching, the parents, feeling that there was nothing further they could do, went to bed.

The next morning, her body was found.

Her friend Sarah had been the last of her friends and family to see her alive. She had stood on the side of the road and watched as Tracey crossed Great North Rd. Then she had turned, walked home and had gone to bed.

While the world slept, Tracey was being murdered.

The post mortem confirmed that the cause of death was strangulation. It was probable that before being strangled she had been struck, as there was a small bruise on her forehead.

The pathologist also discovered small incisions on Tracey's feet which, it was believed, might have been caused by rats while her body was lying on the ground overnight.

The DSIR report did not determine whether Tracey had been sexually assaulted. There was no evidence of seminal stains on her body, on the clothes or in the area where the body was found. The time of death was set at between 10 pm and midnight.

The police began to build up a picture of Tracey's contacts. During the course of this, the police also inevitably built up a profile of the victim.

The parents of Tracey's boyfriend remembered her as a quiet, blonde girl who used to visit their home at weekends and not say anything. "She used to blush if you talked to her."

But her teachers at school painted a slightly different picture. They described Tracey as being of above-average intelligence and always well presented. Her speaking voice was very clear and pleasant, though some believed she put on airs with her English accent. They said she had a strong personality and liked to get her own way, being temperamental and inclined to sulk.

Henderson High School was one of the first of the new co-educational schools that mixed boys and girls in the same environment. But, ironically, it appeared that Tracey Patient did not mix that well with girls and was far more popular with the boys.

She also had many boyfriends, dismissing the current one as soon as a new one took her fancy. Those friendships she did have with other girls, according to the girls interviewed, consisted of her relating her adventures with boys and their attempts at intimacy, which she successfully repelled. She had been very specific about relating her amorous adventures with boys to the other girls and had named names.

Tracey also got on the wrong side of the teachers. Two days before she was murdered, one of the teachers asked her to remain after class for wearing too much make-up. The teacher told Tracey that though the school did not have rules against make-up per se, she did consider that the wearing of eye shadow and false eyelashes by a 13-year-old was beyond what was acceptable. Tracey had told the teacher she would adorn her face as she wished. She then stormed out of the room.

At first, the police inquiries centred on Tracey's 16-year-old boyfriend. He was of below-average intelligence but old enough to drive a car. He had only a vague alibi for the time of the murder, but no material evidence came to light against him.

The inquiry fanned out to include her past boyfriends, many of whom received unflattering comments from Tracey's older sister, Debbie. It was also discovered that Tracey often rode in boys' cars.

Slowly, from a morass of statements, many of which seemed to contradict each other, the police were able to chart the last known movements of Tracey Patient.

At 7.15 pm, she had phoned a close friend called Sally to go out with her, but Sally had declined as she had just received a new sewing machine and she wanted to stay in and use it.

Instead, at 7.30 pm, Tracey left her house to walk to her friend Sarah's home. She spent some time at Sarah's house in Chilcott Rd before phoning her parents at 9 pm to say she was coming home. Sarah walked with her as far as the Henderson Police Station at the corner of Great North Rd and Edmonton Rd. She saw her friend cross the road and then waved her goodbye. Tracey apparently hurried away down the street because she was meant to be home by 9.30 and also probably because it was getting dark.

There was a contradictory sighting of Tracey from another friend who, at about 9 pm on the evening of 29 January, was standing outside the Central Billiard Saloon in Great North Rd, waiting to catch a bus home. The friend had left school and was working as a shop assistant. According to her statement made to the police:

"I saw Tracey go past me in a car. She was sitting in the front passenger's seat. The car had come from the top of Corbans Hill and went down Railside Avenue towards the Pioneer Tavern. The car had stopped at a red light. I heard her call out to me. I know her voice. She leaned across the driver and waved out to me. She just called out '[witness's name]'. I saw that it was Tracey and waved back. I did not see what she was wearing. I know that she sometimes wears her hair in a ponytail, but it was out as I could see it on the back of her shoulders.

"Three weeks earlier, Tracey gave me a silver ring with a 'T' on it. Tracey was in a Mark 2 Zephyr painted a bluey-grey colour. The driver was a Pakeha aged about 16 or 17 with brown hair which went down to his shoulders. It was wavy."

But the youth had not turned to look at the witness and she had not seen his face.

At 9.30 pm, Sarah went home. At about this time, a witness saw a girl walking along the footpath beside Great North Rd. The footpath was below the street level. He only glanced at her but he was surprised that someone so young should be walking alone late at night. He specifically remembered her long blonde hair.

Further along the road, a blue Leyland was parked with a man sitting in the driver's seat. At first, the witness thought it was a traffic officer's car, but this was unlikely as it had only one working headlight. A check by the police revealed that there was no record that a traffic officer's car had been in the vicinity at that hour.

Tracey was last seen alive outside the Henderson Police Station in Great North Rd just after 9.30 pm. She stopped a couple who were walking their dogs to ask them the time.

Also about that time, a girl answering Tracey's description was seen running up Great North Rd by a post office lineman. He saw her get into a car before it drove away.

Just before 10 pm that evening, a local couple were riding their motorcycles along a one-way road past the Waitakere dam. They stopped at the crest of the hill to admire the view, and the lights of their motorcycles came to rest on a car which was parked only a few yards away.

The car was a white Morris Minor and there was a blonde girl sitting in the passenger seat. The car pulled away at the same time as they did and they followed it down Scenic Drive to where it parked at the top of the lookout. The driver's door was open and they again saw the blonde girl sitting inside it.

From the description they gave, the police were certain they had seen Tracey Patient, probably the last people to see her alive – except for the murderer.

Over the next few days the police followed up many leads, some of them bizarre.

A cream or white car was found abandoned in a reserve

by a North Shore woman. Through the windows she could see soiled women's underwear and photographs of a young blonde girl. The police found a driver's licence which belonged to a man who lived in the Waitakere Ranges. However, further police investigation discounted him from the inquiry.

The police were also looking for a 1967 cream or white Mark 2 Cortina which had been seen in the area by a teenage girl out jogging about the time Tracey had disappeared. The jogger had been followed by the car for about a kilometre before she shrugged him off by leaving Great North Rd and cutting through the Henderson Primary School grounds. She said she arrived home at 9.30 pm, just before Tracey would have been on that same stretch of road. The driver made no attempt to speak to the jogger. She estimated that he was in his 20s.

The police were also looking for a tall man in a small car who was standing by the lay-by about the time the body would have been dumped there on the morning of 30 January.

Another suspect was a man seen pestering three women in the area four days before Tracey died. An identikit picture of him was circulated. He was described as a European aged between 28 and 30. He was about 1.75m tall and was said to be good looking with an olive complexion and close-set eyes. His short, well-groomed, black hair had a distinctive parting.

The three women were in a car when the man approached them and offered them a ride in his car. Then he followed one of them on foot.

The man was driving a 1970-71 metallic bronze Hillman Hunter (or possibly a Ford Escort), with a racing-type steering wheel, which was smaller than the usual steering wheel and padded around the rim. The car was upholstered in black. It had a radio fitted below the left parcel tray and two stereo speakers mounted in the rear.

On 29 March, the man was picked up for questioning

after one of the teenage girls he had pestered recognised him in his Hillman Hunter. She quickly jotted down the number of his car and handed it to the police.

He was arrested on a separate charge of assaulting a woman on 26 January. The Hillman Hunter was impounded and closely examined by DSIR scientists but no incriminating evidence was discovered. After the man's account of his movements on the night Tracey disappeared had been checked, he was released and eliminated from the inquiry.

On 3 March, police thought they had a promising new lead when a woman contacted a Youthline counsellor after watching the Police 5 television programme and said that she had been on the road that night tinkering with her car which had broken down. She said a blonde girl had run across the road and disappeared in the direction of what she believed to be a school. A little later, the girl reappeared in the company of a man who was wearing a brown suit. They both got into a brown car and the car drove away.

The woman said she had been reticent to come forward because she had been discouraged from getting involved by her husband. The police asked her to contact them and guaranteed her anonymity but she made no contact and it could not be determined if her sighting was genuine.

Yet another lead that came to nothing concerned a Mark 111 Ford Zephyr that had been outside a hamburger bar in Edmonton Rd at about 9.40 pm on 29 January. There had been two boys and two girls in it and one of the girls fitted the description of Tracey. It appeared to a passerby that the boy had been restraining her when she had tried to get out of the car. The next day, the occupants of the car phoned the police and told them it had just been a lark. They were eliminated from the inquiry.

Tracey's body was retained for three weeks after her death by the Auckland deputy coroner, H. Israel. The police

News Media Auckland

The Identikit picture of a man suspected of the murder of Tracey Patient. He was later contacted but discounted.

had taken all her clothes for examination so her mother had to buy new clothes for her daughter to be buried in.

On 3 March, a memorial service was held at St Michael and All Angels Anglican Church in Henderson. Many of Tracey's school friends attended. At the back of the church, Tracey's boyfriend, who had at first come under suspicion, sat alone. His head was bowed as he left the service and there were tears on his cheeks.

The next day, the Patient family left for England, leaving behind a murder inquiry that was still struggling to find a major lead. Tracey left with them in a coffin and she was buried in a London cemetery.

For the first two years in England, as they struggled to rebuild their lives, Tracey's parents read the New Zealand papers and regularly wrote to the police to see if there had been any developments.

June Patient got a job working at a building society. One day, by a strange quirk of fate, she was suddenly reminded of the tragedy. A man with a New Zealand accent came into the building and when June started talking to him she was shocked to discover that he was the son of the man who had found Tracey's body.

In New Zealand, though little headway was made in finding the murderer, long after Tracey's body had been found there continued to be new twists in the saga.

Fifteen months after the murder, a young man was cleaning his van in order to sell it, when he came across a map which had Tracey's name and address written inside the back cover. He had only owned the van since February of that year. The police spoke to the two previous owners, but the owner at the time of the murder was never found.

Then, in 1977, one of Tracey's possessions suddenly turned up in strange circumstances. When she had walked out of her house to visit her friend Sarah on 29 January 1976, she had been wearing an unusual ring. It was a thin band with a heart shape on the front of it on which the initials JP or JD had been inscribed. The exact initials were uncertain, as the ring had been given to Tracey by a boyfriend who had found it.

When her body was discovered in bush the following day, the ring was not on her finger.

At 9.20 pm on 22 November 1977, a man called the Henderson Police Station. He refused to give his name but he told the policeman on duty that a "broken band" was lying in a rubbish basket in the Avondale shopping centre. The police discovered some tissue paper in a waste basket. When they unwrapped it, they found Tracey Patient's heart-shaped ring.

The previous owner of the ring subsequently contacted the police to tell them that the copper-plate initials were definitely JP.

There was a theory that the person who had made the call and put the ring in the waste basket was not the murderer, but someone who knew who he was. The police offered indemnity against prosecution for anybody who had material evidence who was not a principal offender, but no one came forward.

It was not known at the time that the anonymous caller who had phoned to give police the location of the ring had also given information about a mysterious number he said would unlock the mystery. The number was 126040.

Two years later, the police decided to release the information about the number on a Police 5 show. The telephone lines were soon blocked as callers phoned in with opinions about what the mysterious numbers meant.

Police investigated the numbers of retail accounts, bank accounts, telephones, post office boxes and even social welfare numbers, all to no avail.

So who was the caller? Was he a hoaxer, an associate of the murderer or the murderer himself?

Ten years after her little sister died, Debbie Patient sent an open letter from England to the man who had phoned in the clue about the ring:

"To you, whoever you are.

Ten years ago on 29 January 1976, my sister, Tracey Patient, was murdered. She was 13 years old. The murderer was never caught. But you know who did it, don't you?

You also know that person is evil and should be in prison, so he cannot kill again.

You must want him (I believe it is a man; no woman would have been able to overpower Tracey) caught or you would not have made those anonymous telephone calls.

Why can't you ring again and tell the police this monster's name? Is he your husband? Your son? Is that reason enough to let a murderer walk free?

Who knows, he may kill again, and this time you, or someone you love, may be his victim. How would you feel if he murdered your child?

Tracey has been dead for 10 years but we still miss her so much. We can't help wondering what she would be like now, if that animal you know had not murdered her.

She may have been married, with children of her own. She did not deserve to die.

How can you live with yourself KNOWING who killed her?

Have you got a heart? You must feel something, or you would not have made those calls.

Please, if you have any self-respect, any conscience, any feelings of humanity, give that murderer up."

Debbie Patient

In 1989, the police returned another ring which had been on Tracey's body to the Patient family. It was in the form of a silver threepenny piece and had been given to Tracey by her grandmother before leaving Britain.

Every second Sunday, John and June Patient get up early to buy fresh flowers and put them on Tracey's grave. On the anniversary of Tracey's murder, her sister Debbie writes poems to her dead sister and places them on her grave.

The greatest difficulty the police had in the investigation was that they did not know where Tracey had been murdered. No sticks similar to the one that was knotted in the pantyhose were found within 100 metres of her body and it was believed that she had been murdered elsewhere, possibly in a car, and her body dumped.

We will never know what happened for certain but a clairvoyant who said she had been in communication with Tracey's spirit provided one plausible scenario.

According to her, Tracey had been rushing to get home when a car had slowly drawn up beside her and the driver asked the way to her street. Concerned that she was late, Tracey had climbed into the car without properly inspecting the man. But when she told the man he had driven too far, he didn't slow down, but kept driving.

What seems certain is that Tracey got into a car. As the post mortem results, which said that she died after 10 o'clock, and the evidence of the couple riding bikes showed, from the fact that she did not put up a struggle it can be assumed that she got into the car willingly. Whether she knew the driver is less certain. Possibly she did, but it also seems that she was used to driving around in her boyfriends' cars and therefore might not have thought anything of getting into a passing car.

Her partial state of undress implies that her murderer had sexually assaulted her or was about to, though it is unclear if Tracey was conscious or unconscious at this point. If she was unconscious, it might have resulted from the blow to the side of her head.

Though it is possible that the blow was an accident, it probably wasn't. As the pantyhose that were found around Tracey's neck did not belong to her, the murderer must have brought them with him, which implies some degree of premeditation.

There has also been a theory that the murderer was a woman and a lesbian. No evidence exists to support or refute this.

And what about the ring? Did the murderer take it from her finger when she was dead or alive? The likelihood is that it was when Tracey was alive and that she gave it willingly. For almost two years he, or someone who knew him, held onto it before depositing it in a bin in a very public place.

Why? Was it some sort of attempt at atonement?

It's likely that we will never know. The officer in charge of the inquiry, Detective Inspector Bruce Scott, believes the police never made contact with the killer.

The tragedy is that the killer made contact with Tracey.

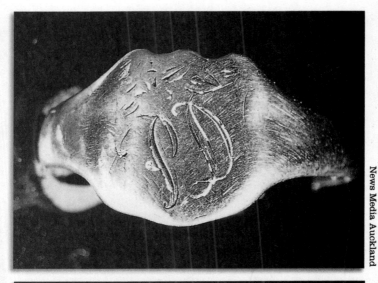

News Media Auckland

Tracey Patient's ring. Did the murderer hold onto it for two years?

7. Alfred Anderson

Who Was the Woman in the Leopard Skin Coat?

All was not what it at first seemed when the body of a retired man was discovered in his Hastings St flat in the Christchurch suburb of Waltham in 1982.

On 4 June of that year, 62-year-old Alfred Anderson's son called at his father's flat to have lunch with him, accompanied by his wife and young child.

When his father failed to answer the knocks on the door, the son forced his way into the house to find his father dead in his lounge, which was spattered with blood. Anderson was lying on his living room floor with a bed cover tossed over him. Underneath it, he was dressed only in underwear and a dressing gown.

Anderson's flat was one of a block of four and the murder sent fear through the other occupants of the flats. One woman had shifted out of her flat and moved in with friends. Two other neighbours had stayed on, but they barricaded their doors. One of them, a Mrs White, wedged a chair against the front door when she went to bed. "I don't know how anyone could have done such a thing," she said. "Alfie was such a lovely chap. He wouldn't hurt a fly."

The other neighbour had used pieces of wood to jam into the sliding doors to ensure they would be secure. Both were grateful that the police maintained a 24-hour presence as the investigation got underway.

Anderson had suffered a violent assault. He had cut and stab wounds to the throat and severe injuries to the left side of his head. It was the cutting of his throat with a sharp instrument which had caused his death.

Anderson's wallet was found on his bedroom floor. It contained no money. His gold wristwatch was also missing. He had bought the watch on a trip to England in 1980. He had been seen wearing the watch earlier that day and as it was not to be found in the flat, it was assumed the killer had taken it. There were no signs that anything else had been taken from the flat.

Anderson had come to Christchurch from England with his family when he was a small child. For the last seven and a half years, ever since his wife died, he had lived alone.

At first, the police believed he might have been killed for the $800 he had recently been paid for a painting job. That money was supposed to go towards a trip he was planning to make to England.

He had gone back there three or four years before, visited his 84-year-old brother and some of his cousins and generally had a good time. He had been due to leave for England on 29 June. The police theory was that Anderson might have discussed the trip and the money he had made with the wrong person who, believing that he kept the money at home, had decided to rob him. Then in the course of the robbery, Anderson had been murdered.

The police began to make inquiries in the locality and made a thorough search of the neighbourhood for the murder weapon. Waste land and gardens in the district were searched for the "sharp instrument" which, it was believed, had caused Anderson's death.

No one in the area had been aware that the murder had taken place until the police cars had converged on the street the next day. An elderly couple lived in a house that backed onto Anderson's flat and their bedroom was only a few metres from his. Yet they heard nothing unusual on that Friday night.

Police said Anderson had told members of his family that he intended going to the movies that night if it was not too cold. A ticket stub found in his flat confirmed that he had indeed spent his last evening at the Odeon Theatre.

Patrons of the cinema were interviewed to see if any of them recalled the old man who probably sat alone that night in the darkness of the auditorium. One witness came forward who saw Anderson talking to a man in the theatre foyer. But the man was never identified.

After the film, Anderson walked home, taking a short cut through the foyer of Christchurch Railway Station. Five people who were waiting in the railway station late on the evening of 2 June responded to the police call for information. Three of them were parents waiting to pick up their children from the West Coast railcar. They were able to positively identify Anderson walking alone through the railway station at about 11.35 pm.

Detectives calculated it would have taken Anderson 25 minutes to walk from the station and arrive at the block of flats where he lived a few hundred metres away at the corner of Hastings St and Waltham Rd. He would have arrived home at about midnight.

At about 12.30 am, a young woman who was walking down the street saw a young man race from Anderson's flat. He was about 25 years old, tall and slim with dark hair. He was wearing a jacket, gathered at the waist, with a light-coloured horizontal band around the left sleeve.

He ran down an alleyway beside shops at the intersection of Hastings St and Waltham Rd to where a 1963 or 1964 Ford Falcon station wagon was parked. The vehicle had one door painted an odd colour.

The young man talked to the driver of the station wagon and then the vehicle sped away.

Two other men were sighted at the scene, whom the police sought to interview. Details of both these men were at first withheld for reasons the police refused to release.

Later, the second man was revealed to be a Maori in his early 20s, about 1.6m in height, and of slight build. He was wearing blue jeans and a waterproof jacket. This man spoke to the young woman who saw the "running man".

The third man the police sought was a European in his late 20s with long fair hair. He was wearing a suit. This man was seen to be behaving suspiciously. He walked along the street near Anderson's flat and then turned around and retraced his steps.

None of the men came forward or was located.

Police widened the inquiry to check up on every person who might have a tendency to commit such a brutal crime. Lists of known knife-wielders were drawn up and their movements for that evening checked.

The day before Anderson was murdered, he was seen talking to a mystery woman in the Northland shopping mall. Shortly afterwards, he was again seen in the company of the same woman outside the Papanui Post Office. She was described as having mousey hair and a three-quarter-length leopard skin coat.

An enormous amount of publicity was generated in the attempt by the police to locate this woman.

Public interest was high and there was a tremendous

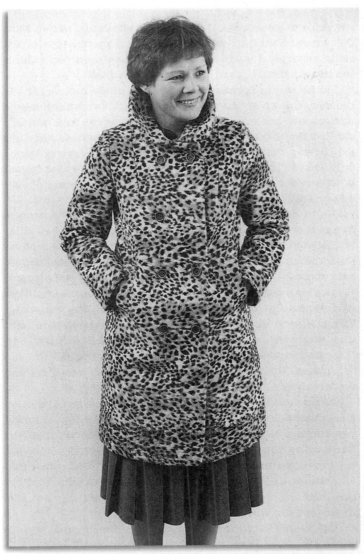

News Media Auckland

A coat similar to the one the mystery woman was seen in.

response to the appeal. The names of about 20 women were put forward and all were investigated, though the police sadly reported that in some cases it had been "stretching the imagination" to call the coats "leopard skin".

Robbery was regarded as the most likely motive for the murder, but if so it was unsuccessful. Investigations of Anderson's bank records revealed that he had already banked the $800 he had been paid for the private painting job. It was probable that Anderson's wallet had contained only small change. The police were suspicious that it had been emptied and discarded on the floor to deliberately leave a false trail.

As there were no signs of a forced entry at Anderson's home, it was possible that Anderson had known his killer and invited him or her in of his own free will. A few months after the killing, the police believed they had stumbled onto an important clue when Anderson's gold watch was found.

Workers painting the roof of a house about 200m from Anderson's flat found the watch lodged in the guttering. There was no doubt the watch belonged to Anderson as it was engraved with his initials, but it elicited no new information to lead the police any closer to the killer.

A year after the murder, the crime was unsolved and Anderson's flat remained empty.

It was several years later when Crimewatch did an enactment of the case that the illusion of the lonely pensioner was finally put to rest. It turned out that, far from being lonely, Anderson lived an active if somewhat underground social life. He was revealed to be a bisexual who had been known to frequent the normal haunts of the gay community of the time such as public toilets, and also to pay for sex with female prostitutes.

On the night of the murder, the two films he had been to see at the Odeon Theatre were Emmanuelle in America and Playbirds. Both were X-rated. The day after the television programme was aired, police came in for some criticism for revealing the details of Anderson's private life, but they said it was a necessary step in order to try to catch the murderer.

At the time of the murder, people involved in the gay community had been reluctant to come forward with information as at the time homosexuality was against the law. It was possible that the woman in the leopard skin coat had been a prostitute whose services Anderson had used. But did he use them the night he died?

The killer or killers of Alfred Anderson have never been caught. The police simply did not have enough evidence which might have led to any feasible lines of inquiry. They were not helped by the grey world that the pensioner inhabited – the massage parlours and the public toilets where he exercised his sexual preferences.

It is possible that his appetite was aroused after having watched the double bill of sex movies at the cinema. On returning home, he may have phoned a man or woman, friend or prostitute, to share the rest of the evening with him. He stripped down to his underwear and clothed himself only in a dressing gown.

Then he answered the knock at the door, opening it to a smiling face. But how long before the smile turned ugly? And for what reason? Was Anderson killed for money, for some sort of personal vendetta or for some other reason?

The attacker had first bludgeoned him with his fist or some blunt instrument and then, while he was semi-conscious, leant over him and slit his throat. Murder was intended and perhaps premeditated. It is possible the killer brought the murder weapon with him or her.

If it was the young man who ran down the alleyway, it seems probable he would have had accomplices. These men might have had Anderson marked as an easy target for some time. He was old and frail, his dalliances carried him to the other side of the law, and he lived alone. But if they were after money, they were disappointed.

And if the motive wasn't money, what was it? The old man seemed to have nothing else to offer them except his life.

8. Kirsa Jensen

A Ride Along
the Beach

Kirsa Jensen was a teenage girl from Napier who was mad about horses. The first horse she owned was called Old Paint because his natural colours looked as if someone had thrown paint all over him. She renamed him Karis to match her own name.

Old Paint was bought when Kirsa's father, the Rev Dan Jensen, was the vicar at St Stephen's Church in Opotiki, which was the scene of a notorious murder. There, in March 1865, the Rev Carl Sylvius Volkner was shot and hanged by a local Maori chief, Kereopa Te Rau. Volkner's head was then cut off, dried in the smoke of a fire and his eyes were eaten by Te Rau. Others joined in and drank Volkner's blood.

Te Rau was executed for the murder in 1872. Three other men had already been executed for the murder in 1866, though one of them, Mokomoko, was later given a posthumous pardon because his only crime was that the rope used to hang Volkner had belonged to him.

More than a century later, Volkner's blood still stained the floor of the church, until it was sanded off a few years before Dan Jensen became the pastor, to encourage Maori people to return to worship.

Later, Dan Jensen was invited to become the minister at St Augustine's Church in Napier after the previous vicar had resigned unexpectedly. The posting seemed to be one made in heaven for a young girl like Kirsa who loved horses. Not only did the new vicarage have a paddock, but there was also another paddock next door on the adjoining YMCA grounds.

Just before the family moved to Napier, Kirsa was offered a 12-year-old grey pony called Kathy. She reluctantly sold Karis, whom she had outgrown, and soon after the family had settled in Napier the horse was transported to their new home. She rode Kathy in a gymkhana and won first prize, but by her 14th birthday she had outgrown her too.

Two months later, in January, she saw another horse advertised in the paper, this time for $400. It was a five-year-old chestnut thoroughbred with a white blaze and three white socks and which stood sixteen hands high.

When Kirsa saw the horse, it was love at first sight. He was called Commodore, but that was soon shortened to "Commo". Over the next few months, she got to know the horse, riding it often and keeping it well groomed.

The first of September is traditionally the first day of spring. That morning in 1983 was a sunny Thursday. Kirsa woke early, showered and had breakfast. In two days' time, she would be competing in a gymkhana with Commodore and that afternoon she planned to ride along the beach to exercise him.

News Media Auckland

Just a young girl who was
mad about horses.

Kirsa gave the horse a final groom before she left. "Bye" was her final word to her mother as she rode off towards the beach. It was 2.45 pm.

She should have been home at about five o'clock. At that hour, the warm sunshine began to fade outside and a chill came over the house, prompting Kirsa's mother, Robyn, to light the fire. She waited for her daughter to return. Kirsa went out riding several times a week and only once had she ever been late home. Then she had ridden straight up to the kitchen window to apologise.

By 5.10, her mother was starting to get worried. There was a noise at the back door but it wasn't Kirsa. It was Kirsa's brother Michael. Now panic was starting to set in. Together they went out to look for Kirsa along the green belt that she would have taken on her way back from the beach. But there was no sign of her. They began to fear that something was desperately wrong.

Kirsa's father arrived home at 6 pm, half an hour later than he was expected. Anxiety clouded his face when he was told Kirsa had not returned. "Which beach?" he asked.

No one knew.

They went out to look for her. Friends were phoned and went out searching too. They could find no sign of Kirsa or Commodore.

At 6.45 pm, distraught and worried, they phoned the police. When a policeman arrived shortly afterwards, he told them a horse, which turned out to be Commodore, had been found running free on the Waitangi Bridge which crossed the Tutaekuri River. It was near a fertiliser plant whose chimneys ominously belched smoke continuously into the air. The plant was next to the Hastings road. On the other side, scrub led down to the Awatoto beach. The search quickly centred on that area.

It was led by a local policeman, Sergeant Howard Carseldine, who lived just across the road from the vicarage. He was one of the last people to talk to Kirsa. As he had walked to work for the afternoon shift, she had been grooming Commodore. He had said "hello" to her.

The searchers were spaced out into long lines, walking shoulder to shoulder across the beach lit by portable lights powered by a generator.

Two rivers fed into the inlet next to the sea, the Tutaekuri and the Ngaruroro. Their banks were searched, as were the sand dunes and the beach and an area of open land known as the Colenso reserve.

On the Awatoto beach was a gun emplacement. It had been built during the Second World War for an enemy attack that never came. The roof had collapsed, the concrete walls were stained and weeds grew out of the corners. Here the searchers found part of a bridle.

Near the Tutaekuri River they found hoof-prints. They were in a circle and there was a mark in the sand as if something heavy had been dragged through them. From these the police surmised that Commodore had reared, causing Kirsa to fall off and drown.

Police and friends scoured the area until it was too dark to see. The search was called off at 11.30 pm. Commodore returned to the vicarage that night, walked home by Kirsa's brother Michael and a friend. A traffic officer walked before them holding a torch, lighting their way through the darkness.

Kirsa's mother could not sleep that night. At one point, she picked up a Bible and opened it at random. Her eyes fell on a quotation which read, "I shall bring honour to Christ, whether I live or die. For what is life? To me it is Christ. Death will bring more."

What did it mean? Was Kirsa telling her that she was dead?

The search resumed just before 6 am the next morning. The tide had come in during the night and washed away the circle of hoof-prints in the sand.

The police put boats into the river to search for Kirsa's body while both a helicopter and a Tiger Moth donated by a local pilot buzzed overhead, sweeping the area for any sign of her. A heat-sensing device was attached to a helicopter which combed the area and, though one hot spot was detected, nothing significant was found there.

Blood was found on grass, pieces of glass and sticks lying on the ground near the gun emplacement. The searchers were called back and the area cordoned off as the hunt turned into a murder inquiry.

A tarpaulin was placed over the gun emplacement and a night watch posted. Gridlines were set up three feet apart with twine so the area could be thoroughly searched, and rows of policemen crawled through the grids on their hands and their knees, sifting the sand in front of them for clues.

Broken pieces of leather from Commodore's bridle were found on the beach. These were pieced together with the part of the bridle that had been found the night before. The throat lash was in three pieces and both the cheekstraps were broken, indicating that some violent activity had taken place.

When Commodore had been found he was still wearing a noseband with the martingale secured to it. The reins had been with the bridle, but the martingale was normally secured to the reins, which implied the reins had been undone at some stage.

On the bit was a ring with a piece of rope attached to it. The same type of rope was found attached to a rusting piece of reinforcing bar sticking out of the gun emplacement on the seaward side. Later, blood was found on the rope. When tested, the blood type was found to be the same as Kirsa's.

So Commodore must have been tied there at some stage. But who had done it? Even if Kirsa had a good reason to tie Commodore up, she would never have secured her beloved horse by the nose bit.

A distinctive 30cm scratch was discovered on Commodore's saddle. Kirsa had long, strong fingernails and the scratch seemed to indicate that her hand had ridden down the saddle as she had been prevented from mounting Commodore.

Strands of blonde hair which went down to their roots were discovered near where the blood had been found. It was taken away to be tested against hair taken from Kirsa's hairbrush. When the police dusted Kirsa's room for fingerprints, they found some on her school folders, but then had to take fingerprints from teachers at her school to eliminate their prints from the inquiry.

Some of Kirsa's blood was found on Commodore. He also had a small nick on his hindquarters. The DSIR took some of Commodore's hair for testing and on their behalf the vet took hoof scrapings. Blood was discovered as far as 26 metres away from the gun emplacement. No traces of semen were found.

When she disappeared, Kirsa had been wearing an Astrosonic digital watch, that had been ordered for her

News Media Auckland

The ominous gun emplacement. The flags
mark bloodstains.

through a mail order catalogue. A second one had been
ordered at the same time for a friend of the family. That
watch was borrowed by the police to help them with their
search.

As the hours of Kirsa's disappearance began to turn into
days, there was still some hope that Kirsa would be found.
A reward was offered which eventually reached $31,000.
Her face appeared on television and in newspapers, and the
police made appeals over the radio. Videos of the search
were played in 20 stores in Napier and Hastings, with
people blocking the footpaths to watch them.

Many people called the police in response. A flood of
letters also unleashed a variety of advice. One was from an
inmate at Paremoremo Maximum Security Prison in
Auckland, which said, "May the Almighty Shepherd find

the little lamb and bring her home." Others were not so encouraging. One suggested that if the police watched out for hovering seagulls, the body would be found below them.

An anonymous call had come in on the first Sunday afternoon of the search. A woman had said that she was travelling along the stretch of road where Kirsa was last seen and she saw a man with Kirsa at the gun emplacement who was trying to kiss her. An appeal was made for the woman to come forward but she never did.

Clairvoyants and psychics also responded with advice about where to dig. One was Andrew Narain, a yogi from Greymouth. He claimed that Kirsa had been abducted by a Maori who lived in a derelict house, and he had thrown her body into the river. He said the man had recently traded his 1964 blue Zephyr for a white ute. Neither the man nor the derelict house was discovered.

Another more practical piece of advice said:

"I believe I have to write this letter to you. I once owned a dapple-grey mare for five years and I knew that horse as much and as well as she knew me. Please read my letter as it is important as the Lord, he asked me to write to you.

Firstly, you must get somebody to ride the horse over exactly the same roads etc as Karen say did. I use that name as I don't know or remember her name.

1st You must get somebody to ride the horse over the same roads etc Karen did.

2nd Whoever rides the horse must call him/her by name, and tell the horse what you are going to do and why.

3rd If the horse
a. Shied
b. got a fright
c. was frightened
Then in all cases he will be timid when coming

**up to the same place again. This might sound
silly but horses are very intelligent, and they
know more than we think they do.**

**It is also important that the person knows how
to ride the horse and gets the trust of the horse
and is not scared of horses.**

**I pray and hope that when the horse does shy or
whatever that you will have the police dog there,
as I am sure the Lord will work through the
horse.**

**PS. Don't forget to give the horse a carrot and a
good-sized piece of sugar as a reward. This might
be one thing you have not tried but it is
worthwhile."**

The letter was to prove uncannily accurate when
Commodore was returned to the gun emplacement for a re-
enactment, ridden by a friend of Kirsa. Afterwards the
horse fell sick, presumably from colic from grass that had
been cut and then left to ferment. But the horse had been
reluctant to return to the gun emplacement. The animal
was a mute witness to whatever had occurred there.

Police believed they might have finally discovered
Kirsa's remains when human bones were washed up on a
nearby beach, but it turned out they came from a Maori
burial ground.

Not one drop of rain fell during September as the search
for Kirsa went on. The most likely and unlikely places were
searched for her body including offal pits, the sluice pipes
of the nearby Whakatu freezing works, which went out to
sea, and the local shingle works. The piles of shingle were
moved and probed to see if her body was hidden
underneath.

For all of September, the back door of the vicarage was
left unlocked and the outside light on in the hope that by
some miracle Kirsa would reappear. Her family had

continued to hope that she had stumbled and fallen and become disoriented and she would somehow stagger home tired and weary and fall into loving arms. The hunt for her that had begun on the first day of the month was officially called off on the last day of the month.

All hope of finding her alive had gone. The back door was locked that night.

Family and friends still spent their Sundays searching for the body. Armed with spades, they went to wild bushy areas nearby where she could have been buried. They dug up any place that looked as if it might be a likely burial ground or showed evidence of turned soil.

As it grew more and more unlikely that Kirsa's body would be found, the police intensified their search for the murderer. They reconstructed the last confirmed sightings of her on the day she had disappeared.

At 3.12 pm, a witness saw a girl with blonde hair riding a horse south along Te Awa Avenue, Napier. Between about 3.15 and 3.30 pm, Kirsa and Commodore were seen crossing State Highway 2 towards the beach. At about 3.30 pm, they were seen passing the Certified Concrete plant at Awatoto.

Ten minutes later, a witness driving past Awatoto beach noticed several vehicles near a gun emplacement, including a white utility. Five minutes later, two witnesses saw Kirsa and Commodore beside the gun emplacement. Other witnesses saw her exercising her horse on the beach over the next 10 minutes.

Two of them were young surfers. They saw a large horse ridden by a blonde girl who was dressed in blue jeans and a blue windbreaker. They passed her as they paddled out to sea. She was about 20 metres away and she smiled back at them when they waved at her.

A witness saw Kirsa at 4 pm on his way home from work at the fertiliser plant. She was galloping Commodore along the high part of the beach. He described her as a Pakeha girl, wearing jeans and a blue top, who had good control of her horse. On the track that led to the gun emplacement, he saw a parked car that he thought was a white Austin.

The surfers' last sighting of the girl was at about 4.15 pm.

At 4.20, an Austin Cambridge with a red stripe down the side arrived at the gun emplacement. Inside were two more surfers. One of them went down to the water's edge while the other climbed on top of the gun emplacement to look at the surf. He saw a blonde girl leading a horse.

The other surfer at the water's edge also saw her. He said her head was tilted forward and she was holding a handkerchief to her face. When she took it away from her face, he could see it was either red or covered in blood. The two friends left soon after.

At about that time, another witness was driving north along State Highway 2 in his cream Austin Cambridge. He saw a girl standing and holding a horse beside the gun emplacement.

He said that a male European, 50 years old, balding and of stout build, was standing near the girl. A white, one-tonne, flat-deck truck with brown sides was parked nearby. At first, he thought it was a Mazda but later, when the police took him to see several trucks, he began to doubt the make, though he was sure it had stained wooden sides.

Another witness driving a Mazda station wagon north along State Highway 2 saw a horse at the gun emplacement. He also saw a European male, approximately 1.8 metres tall, aged about 45 years and of solid build, holding a female against the gun emplacement with an outstretched arm. Parked nearby was a white one-tonne truck with flat deck and brown sides.

At 4.20 pm, Kirsa was seen talking to the driver of a white ute. She had blood over her face. The witness driving the cream Austin Cambridge returned to the gun emplacement area. He spoke to Kirsa and noticed minor injuries to her face. She said she had taken a fall from her horse and someone had gone to get her parents, whom she expected to arrive in 5 to 10 minutes. He left the area.

At 4.40 pm, another man passed along the same road and saw the horse in a state of agitation but did not see anybody else. The horse was tethered to the gun emplacement.

At 4.45 pm, another surfer arrived at the gun emplacement. He saw nobody else there.

Another witness said that at about 4.30 pm he saw a white truck travelling across the Clive Bridge towards Hastings. The driver had his arm around a girl who fitted the description of Kirsa.

At 4.40 pm, a white ute or truck was parked in Colenso Domain. Two minutes later, a white ute was seen at the gun emplacement.

At 5.20 pm, a white ute was seen on the beach side of the road just past the Tutaekuri Bridge towards Clive. At about the same time, a white ute was seen leaving the gun emplacement and heading towards Napier.

Commodore broke free at about 5.30 pm and ran off down the beach. He was found wandering near the Tutaekuri River Bridge at about 6.45 pm.

The police launched one of the biggest manhunts ever mounted in New Zealand at that time. More than 800 white utes were checked. They became so notorious that one owner of a white ute even put a sign on his vehicle which said, "I've been checked by the police."

Suspicion began to fall on the driver of the 1961 cream-coloured Austin Cambridge that had distinctive grey primer paint on the left front mudguard. His name was William John Russell and he was a convicted rapist.

A few years before, he and three other men had abducted a girl outside a post office in Palmerston North, took her into the country and raped her. Russell was sentenced to two-and-a-half-years' imprisonment for the offence. At the beginning of 1983, drunk one night, he had broken into the house of a woman he knew and pulled her out of bed by her hair. He was fined and ordered to pay compensation and costs.

The piece of rope used to tie Commodore to the gun emplacement had broken when he escaped. The two pieces had a total length of about 3.5m – and were of a type known as Feltex Duralene. There was a loop at each end, which implied the rope had previously been used to tie down a load over a vehicle.

There was no salt found on the rope, which ruled out its having been washed up on the beach. Rimu pollens were found on it, however, and rimu is very rare in the Hawkes Bay, tending to grow in more temperate northern regions.

Green sand as well as copper sulphate, a chemical used in orchard spray, was found on the rope. Green sand was also rare in Hawkes Bay. It had been unknown in the region until wells had been drilled. Only two wells had been bored in the district which were known to have produced green sand. One of them had been drilled for water on the property of a local farmer called Ray Durney. William Russell worked for Durney as his orchard manager.

Russell was informed that the debris vacuumed up in his car had contained comparable percentages of pollen and minerals to those on the rope found at the gun emplacement. Fibres found on the rope also matched those on his trousers. In his car, horse hair had also been found, which was chestnut and white, matching the markings of Commodore who was chestnut with white socks. Green sand was also found in the car.

Russell's movements for 1 September were checked. On that day, he had left work at 3.30 pm. After dropping off someone's wages and visiting a hire centre, he said he had been heading home when he decided to visit a nursery in Napier and buy some shrubs for his garden. As he drove past the gun emplacement, he said he saw the girl with the horse. A man seemed to be leading her towards the white truck.

He said he was concerned for her and decided to drive to the gun emplacement. He was on the opposite side of the road, but instead of taking a U turn, he said that because of the fast-moving traffic, he took a back road past the fertiliser works which brought him out near the gun emplacement.

When he got there, the white truck had gone. He said he spoke with the girl. She had blood on her face. He asked her if she was all right. She said she was, and that the horse had shied and she had fallen off. Someone had gone to get her parents.

Next, Russell said, he drove around the gun emplacement and went straight home, changing his mind about paying a call on the friend he had intended to visit.

Russell claimed he actually looked at his watch when he left the gun emplacement and it was exactly 4.30. He said he got home at 4.35 at the latest. But a woman witness said she had seen him at the gun emplacement at 4.40 pm. How accurate was the time of this sighting? The woman had then gone to a butcher's shop to buy some meat. The time printed on the receipt was 4.50 pm. A detective retraced her travel time and found she would have been at the gun emplacement at 4.40 pm as she claimed.

Russell's story was also inconsistent. When he was interviewed by police on 2 September, he said he did not get out of the car. When interviewed on 6 September, he said he had got out to talk to the girl who seemed to him to be about 16 or 17 years old.

When it became known that the police considered Russell the prime suspect, he became a target of abuse. One night someone emptied the contents of a rubbish bin on his driveway.

He reacted by phoning a friend of the Jensen family and said he wanted to talk to him. He also implied that he would be able to unburden himself as the friend was an ordained priest. The friend drove to Russell's house in Whakatu where they talked in the kitchen. Russell was evasive, and every time he was asked a tricky question, he claimed not to remember.

Despite the circumstantial evidence, the police did not

feel the evidence was strong enough to gain a conviction against Russell. The risk was that if he was charged and was acquitted, then according to the law he could never be tried again for the same crime. Then if Kirsa's body turned up later and there was evidence that Russell was involved in her murder, he would be immune from conviction.

The frustrated police were forced to await a body or a confession.

One night, a year after Kirsa had disappeared, her mother, Robyn, was at home convalescing from an operation when there was a knock at the door. She explained what happened in her book "Kirsa: A Mother's Story" which was published in 1994:

"When she answered the door at first she did not recognise the man standing before her.

"Are you sure you don't know who I am?" he asked. She knew his face was familiar but she couldn't place it. He introduced himself. "I'm John Russell."

For 20 minutes, she talked to the man who she suspected had killed her daughter. He made no confession, nor gave any indication of where the body might be buried, even though he told her, "I just want to be free of the guilt of this burden." Angered by the loss of her daughter, Robyn Jensen found the courage to confront him. She told him what she believed had happened at the gun emplacement that day.

"She would have put up a good fight, she would have fought to the bitter end. She was brutally assaulted. She was grabbed by the hair from behind and her head was bashed against the emplacement. That's how the blood got onto the emplacement... I would rather she died than be raped by a bastard."

"She wasn't raped," Russell replied. "She wasn't dead when she was taken from the emplacement..."

Despite his evasiveness, Russell all but confessed to her that he had murdered Kirsa.

Later he appeared on the very first edition of the

"Holmes" show and admitted that he had confessed to the murder twice, though he later retracted these "confessions".

Almost two years after Kirsa disappeared, Russell visited the police station and told police his memory was starting to return. He said he had an image of hitting Kirsa on the head with a rock. She was lying on the ground and he was standing over her.

Still no charges were laid against Russell. A confession can be retracted. It might not even be the truth. Many people have confessed to crimes they never committed.

Russell visited the police station again. This time he said he remembering talking to Kirsa, then she ran away. He chased her and caught her behind the gun emplacement. He recalled hitting her with a stone and burying her under a shrub at Pakowhai Reserve.

The police took him to the reserve and to the shrub. All that remained of it was a stump. The police dug up the area. They also used a metal detector hoping to find Kirsa's watch, but there was no trace of her.

Russell's life began to collapse. His marriage broke up, he had a serious car accident and was committed to Sunnyside Psychiatric Hospital. He made the newspaper headlines when he escaped and was recaptured at Wairoa. He was later transferred to Lake Alice Psychiatric Hospital.

Seven years after she had disappeared, Kirsa Jensen was legally declared dead. Two years later, so was John Russell. Perhaps the burden of his guilt became too much for him. He hanged himself in a Hastings guesthouse. He left no note.

But did he murder Kirsa Jensen on that lonely beach on 1 September 1983? Was a convicted rapist really remorseful enough to go to the aid of a young girl he thought was in trouble? One whom he believed to be 16 or 17 rather than a more sexually immature 14-year-old? Did he take a back road to return to the gun emplacement because he had a misdeed in mind? If she really told him that someone had gone to phone her parents, why did no one come forward to corroborate that?

Why did he look at his watch for the exact time when he left if not to prepare his alibi? And why did a chance encounter with a young girl make him change his mind about visiting his friend? Did he really change his itinerary because something awful happened at the gun emplacement?

That ugly concrete structure was built at a time of war. It was intended to withstand an enemy attack, but was never used, yet it persisted as a place designed for violence and on 1 September 1983 it fulfilled its original purpose. Violence occurred there.

Did Russell see an attractive and vulnerable girl, one who was injured and perhaps a little stunned by a fall from her horse? Did he make sexual advances to her? And when the shy, young teenager rebuffed him and tried to flee, did that trigger some predatory instinct in his deranged mind?

According to his fragmented "confession", he might have attacked her but not killed her at the beach. Then he took her away in his car. Perhaps she died on the journey and he buried her.

The police considered there were several likely locations for the body, including Black Bridge and Chesterhope, both of which were within five minutes' driving distance of both the gun emplacement and Russell's home.

There was one ironic twist if Russell was the murderer. His son was born on exactly the same day as Kirsa.

Today Kirsa Jensen persists as an icon to lost innocence. She lives on through a cup and a scholarship named after her, through a chapel dedicated to her at St Augustine's Church in Napier, and a tree that was planted at the gun emplacement where she was last seen.

Other memorials to her are a clock that stopped at 8.48, the time of her birth and Kirsa's last unfinished diary entry which prophetically read, "Been a long time I know…"

9. Ernie Abbot

Suitcase of Death

At 5.19 pm on 27 March 1984, a massive explosion ripped through the Trades Hall building in Vivian St in the middle of Wellington.

The explosion was so powerful it blew out the sturdy front and back doors of the building. The foyer walls were blistered by the heat and scorched black and doors in the hallway were shattered or blown off their hinges. Wood panelling was smashed and a hole punched through a wall.

Heather Birnie, assistant secretary of the Storemen and Packers Union, was sitting in her Corolla car outside the building at the time of the blast. Such was the force of the explosion that it pushed her car several feet out from the kerb. The caretaker's dog, a dachshund-cross called Patch, was blown through the Trades Hall doors and ended up cowering under her car. Nearby shops were damaged by flying debris. An electrical shop had its windows smashed, doors knocked out of their frames and fluorescent light fittings shattered.

Luckily, at the time of the explosion, the only people on the first floor of the building were two other members of the Storemen and Packers Union. Standing shocked inside their first floor office when the door was blown off its hinges were union secretary Phil Mansor and research officer David Butler. They had been catching up on some paperwork. Butler had just turned on the radio and was tuning into short wave to try to pick up a Spanish radio news bulletin when, as Mansor described later, there was a noise like "an almighty cannon going off".

The office lights went out and a pall of black smoke crept through the corridors of the building. The windows blew in, the door-frame splintered, two windows shattered and the lights went out.

Though Mansor was "shaking like a leaf", both men were unhurt.

Butler looked out the door. "Phil, I think we've just had our first bomb blast," he said. He reached for the phone and dialled 111.

Heather Birnie and her mother, Gladys Thompson, who also worked for the Storemen and Packers Union, had just left the office and gone down in the lift. As the thick pall of smoke was coming from the lift, the two men were fearful that it had been booby-trapped.

Mansor ran down the stairs. There was debris everywhere. Pockets of fire ate at wooden frames and fittings.

Electrical shop proprietor Ron Wiseman, who had an office in the Morehu Hall immediately behind Trades Hall, was being helped across rubble. The blast had showered him with glass and he was dazed.

Then Mansor saw what remained of a body lying on the floor and stood staring at it transfixed. Suddenly a rough hand grabbed him by the scruff of the neck and dragged him towards the street. He turned to look at the man who

News Media Auckland

The scene inside Wellington Trades Hall after the explosion which killed Ernie Abbot.

was holding him. The man was dressed in normal clothes but Mansor quickly surmised that he was a policeman.

"Move, you silly bastard," the plainclothes detective shouted. "There may be another bomb."

Mansor hurried out into the street where he joined the crowd that had quickly gathered. Many of them were trade unionists who had rushed to the scene to see if friends or colleagues were inside.

Though dazed, Butler had gone to search the upper floors of the building to see if anyone was there. When he found the area empty, he made his way out onto a balcony to await the emergency services. They were not long in arriving and he too made his way down through the remains of the foyer out onto the street.

In a matter of minutes, the street was full of police cars, fire engines and ambulances. The building was immediately cordoned off and rush hour traffic redirected. Army bomb experts and sniffer dogs were called in to go through the building and make sure there were no other bombs.

It was first thought that the explosion had been caused by a gas leak, but investigation soon revealed that the supply had been turned off for the summer.

When the building was declared safe, a body, the one Mansor had stared at, lay unidentified in the rubble.

On hearing this news on the radio, one woman feared it might be her boyfriend, who worked at the Trades Hall. She drove from her home in Lower Hutt to find out for herself. Luckily for her, it wasn't.

The body was so badly burned and the injuries were so severe that visual identification was not possible, but it soon transpired that the victim of the blast was the 63-year-old caretaker of the building, Ernie Abbot. He had been the caretaker for the last ten years and was also a past vice-president of the Caretakers, Cleaners and Security Guards Union. Only the year before, he had been made a life member for his service to the union.

Abbot lived in a flat above the Trades Hall with his dog

Patch, which followed him everywhere. Abbot was keen on horse racing and owned shares in several horse racing syndicates. He also enjoyed a flutter, but whenever he won his winnings were generously shared with others.

After one of his bets came in, the staff would arrive the next day to find cakes with their morning tea. The charity the Home of Compassion was also a beneficiary of his good fortune.

Though Abbot was too modest to speak of it, he was also a war hero. When he was serving in the Navy during the Second World War, he had saved another man's life. The man, Donald Campbell, had been serving on the minesweeper The Sargasso in the English Channel in 1943 when it was sunk by a mine. The ship went down in three minutes and Campbell was in the water for three and a half hours before help arrived from the minesweeper Bridport, which Abbot was serving on.

By this stage, Campbell was too exhausted to climb up into the safety of the minesweeper so Abbot reached over and pulled Campbell into the boat by his hair.

Afterwards, Abbot visited Campbell where he was recuperating in hospital in Portsmouth.

Abbot seemed an unlikely individual target for the attack. He was described by the Trades Council vice-president, Geoff Turner, as, "A gentleman, a working man. He was a real Vivian St personality – he liked everybody. He loved a pint and he would chat to the young ladies around Trades Hall."

The Cleaners and Caretakers' Union president, W.J. Knox, said of him, "A kinder man with a greater sense of humour I have yet to see."

The police dusted every centimetre of the wall around the entrance door of the building up to head height for fingerprints. The whole area was photographed to show items in their original positions, then those items were vacuumed up for forensic examination.

The man placed in charge of the 100-man investigation

team was Detective Inspector Ted Lines.

Though murder by bomb is unusual in New Zealand, bombings are not as unusual as is generally believed. The case of James Ward is mentioned earlier in this book.

On 18 November 1982, two years before the Wellington Trades Hall explosion, a 22-year-old "punk activist", Neil Roberts, attempted to blow up the Wanganui Computer Centre. He succeeded only in creating extensive damage to the foyer of the building and killing himself in the attempt.

His death may have been deliberate, as beforehand he had written around the area slogans such as "no future" and "this punk won't see 23".

In May 1976, two Hare Krishna members were killed by an explosion in a shed in Grey Lynn, Auckland, used for manufacturing incense. Police also discovered an unexploded detonator in the debris. It is believed they were manufacturing bombs from fire extinguishers, possibly to blow up abattoirs where cows, sacred to their religion, were being killed.

At the beginning of 1984, an anonymous caller claimed that terrorist groups were being set up in New Zealand to commit acts of violence. A few days later, a Palmerston North sub-branch of the Bank of New Zealand was rocked by an explosion.

It appeared that the Trades Hall explosion had emanated from a suitcase that had been seen on the ground floor of the building during the day of the explosion. It had been put outside the office of the Wellington Tramways Union. The suitcase had been first sighted at 9.40 am and had lain there all day. During that time, some girls decided that they would steal it, but luckily for them they didn't.

At about 5 pm, it had been noticed again by the Wellington Trades Council president, Pat Kelly. He had intended to pick it up and move it himself, but didn't because his hands were full of papers at the time. For him it was a lucky escape.

Even so, he came back a second time to shift it, but just

as he went to do so he was called away to move his car which was blocking a truck. A second lucky escape.

Just after 5 pm, Heather Birnie and her mother, Gladys Thompson, had passed Abbot in the hall. As usual his dog Patch was close by. Mrs Thompson bent down to scratch the dog's belly.

"If you rub my stomach, I'll kick my legs too," joked Abbot.

Nearby was the old suitcase which had been left all day beside a pillar close to the office of the Tramways Union and the printing room. The suitcase had cloth wrapped around the handle and a piece of cloth sticking out of the case. Birnie and Abbot discussed the suitcase, with Abbot concluding: "It's been there all day. I'd better stick it in my office."

The women said goodbye and walked towards Mrs Birnie's car, which was parked outside the front doors of the building. Normally, she parked it in a side street, but she had gone out again earlier that day and left it in front.

They got into the car and shut the doors. As Mrs Birnie turned the ignition, the bomb exploded.

Ernie Abbot took the full force of the blast. His dog, Patch, was picked up and tossed outside, where he was discovered singed and cowering underneath Heather Birnie's car by a passerby. When he was taken to a vet, the dog was found to have been blinded by the flash of the blast. He had sustained lung damage and second degree burns. The dog survived. Unfortunately its owner did not.

Just a few shreds of the deadly suitcase remained.

Whether it was intended to be detonated that way or not, it seems certain the movement of picking up the suitcase had triggered the detonator. When the bomb was reconstructed later, it was found to have an anti-handling device and a timing device to allow the person who deposited the suitcase to get well clear before the bomb exploded.

The anti-handling device was a mercury switch. The way

it worked was that wires from the battery were linked to the detonator via mercury in a glass vial. The mercury would only allow an electrical connection to take place when it was tipped. The mercury would run to the end of the vial, where the electrical wires made the connection.

The starting unit was a type commonly used at that time in industry for large electrical motors. It had been imported from Melbourne between the early 1940s and the late 1960s. The unit had a wide number of uses, and it was believed that about 1000 of them had been imported into the country.

The unit recovered from the wreckage of the Trades Hall showed signs of corrosion and was screwed to a diaphragm unit, which the police believed the bomber obtained at the same time he bought the unit.

The battery, which it was believed had been used to power the bomb's timing device, was an Eveready 509. Police quizzed retailers about recent sales of this type of battery, which were quite unusual as they had not been produced since June 1982 but had a shelf life of up to seven years.

The bomb's construction sounded uncannily like the one described by John Le Carre in his novel "The Little Drummer Girl". In the book, the bomb was hidden inside a battered old suitcase which was filled with wadding to try to hide the bulge of the lethal device inside. In Le Carre's book, the timing device used was a cheap wristwatch.

Two weeks before the explosion, an article appeared in the Australian Post describing a similar occurrence in 1972 in Perth, Australia. A suitcase had been placed in the Department of Employment and Industrial Relations. Inside were a time bomb and a mix of ammonium nitrate and diesel, equivalent to 42 sticks of gelignite.

The caretaker of the building, 60-year-old William Anderson, pulled apart the wire between the clock and the bomb only minutes before it was due to go off. The bomb was powered by the same battery utilised in the Trades Hall bombing.

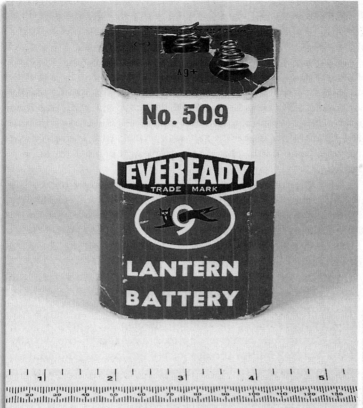

News Media Auckland

The type of battery used in the Trades Hall bomb.

The police used descriptions from witnesses to build up a composite image of the suitcase placed in the Trades Hall. From these, it appeared the suitcase could have been a type last manufactured in 1971 and which were once commonly used by school children.

It was estimated to be about 40cm long, made of light green fibrecell material with a mottled black or blue print over the green. It was very faded, worn and bulging, with a folding rather than a hinged handle, which was covered with cloth.

One key piece of the suitcase that had been recovered had a label stuck on it which read, "Rica Banana Bananaboa Ecuador." As Bonita bananas have been traditionally imported into New Zealand, it was believed that the Rica brand might have represented a special order brought into the country to make up for a shortfall. But nobody came forward who could recall sticking such a label on such a suitcase.

The manufacturer of the suitcase was believed to be the Flight Luggage Company. Police were having difficulty finding a similar suitcase and had one specially manufactured. A poster appeal was launched, with about 1000 coloured photographs of the replica of the suitcase distributed, but to no avail.

In the search for the murderer, about 3000 exhibits were taken from the bomb site and inspected by the DSIR, and hundreds of people were interviewed who had been in the Vivian St area at the time of the blast.

A young man had been noticed loitering in the vicinity of the Trades Hall on the day of the explosion. He had been seen by three Trades Hall workers at different times of the day. One worker said he saw the man at about midday and then again at about 4 pm. Another witness said he saw him running away from the Trades Hall immediately after the explosion. The man was described as being of dark complexion, possibly a Maori or Pacific Islander.

Another man was also sought who had been seen walking up and down Vivian, Taranaki and Cuba Sts between about 10.15 and 10.30 am on the Tuesday of the murder. He was then seen walking through that area again between 10.45 and midday.

He was described as a European in his mid-30s who was about 177cm tall with short brown hair. He was well dressed in a blue suit, white shirt and possibly a blue tie.

A man subsequently came forward but was not believed to be the one who had been sighted.

Another man was seen walking up Taranaki St that day carrying a case similar to the one described to have caused the explosion. He was a European in his mid-40s, about 182cm tall, with brown hair which could have been slightly greying. He was wearing dark trousers and jacket that matched but were not necessarily a suit. His trousers were short. One witness described him as "someone trying to look like one of the down-and-out regulars but he did not quite fit the type".

Another man was seen entering Taranaki St at about 9.30 am. He was European in his late 40s, balding, with dark hair. He was also about 182cm tall, and wore a striped, navy-coloured suit and a light, open-necked shirt. He was also carrying a similar suitcase. Because of the similarities in descriptions to the other man with greying hair, police believed both sightings could possibly have been the same man.

At 12.45 pm on that day, a middle-aged man was also seen to throw a suitcase into Wellington harbour from the Jervois Quay footbridge. He was then observed trying to sink it with a stick. The man never came forward and the suitcase was never found by police divers. It transpired that the area was a popular dumping ground for bags after thieves had rifled through them.

When the police issued an identikit picture of a man they wanted to interview, 26 people came forward saying they recognised him.

On 29 March, a call was made to a Wellington radio station, Radio Windy, by a man claiming to be a member of the group that planted the bomb. He said he was "not actually fully involved, but he knew who was". The police recorded the call but were unable to trace the man who had made it.

There was so little to pinpoint why the attack had been made that a whole host of theories proliferated, ranging from the possible to the highly improbable.

One theory was that the attack was aimed at the union movement. At that time, many meetings were taking place to discuss retaliatory action against Muldoon's wage freeze. Later, it was claimed that Muldoon had launched a hate campaign against the unions. It was a time of anti-union feeling, which had been started a few years earlier by the reforms of the union movement instigated by Margaret Thatcher in England.

Many members of the Wellington Trades Council had their offices in the hall but a number of them had gone to the new Labour Party headquarters for a meeting that day. Another meeting had also taken place that day at the Federation of Labour building in Lukes Lane between the Labour Party and the Federation of Labour (FOL), which together comprised the Joint Council of Labour. There was a possibility that meeting had been the target but that the attacker was unaware that the FOL had moved from the Trades Hall to its new headquarters several years before.

Another theory was that the attack was the response to a wildcat strike by bus drivers of the Wellington City Corporation, which had thrown rush hour traffic into chaos the day before. But a bombing did seem an exaggerated form of revenge for a relatively minor problem.

Yet another theory was that the bomb was actually intended for the Nomads gang, which had a work trust office on the first floor of the Trades Hall. The Nomads had been debt-collecting, and it was thought that a debtor with whom they had been heavy handed was seeking revenge, but had got cold feet and left the bomb on the ground floor.

Perhaps more feasible was the theory that the attack was directed against the anti-nuclear protester Dr Helen Caldicott. She was soon to arrive in the country and the bomb went off near the print room in the Trades Hall, which at the time was printing leaflets in anticipation of her arrival.

Other theories were that the bombing had been designed

by a right-wing Asian government opposed to the unions and alternately that a left-wing group was behind the bombing in a misplaced attempt to gain sympathy for the union movement.

The funeral of Ernie Abbot was held on 3 April 1984 in the Wellington Town Hall. As a mark of respect, the Wellington Trades Council paid for his 60-year-old sister, Mrs Ethel Bainbridge, to fly from Liverpool to attend. Also in attendance among the 2500 mourners were his brother from Auckland and a contingent of men who had served with him on the Navy vessel HMNZS Lachlan.

There were no hymns at the service. Ernie Abbot's favourite song, "Sierra Sue", was played and "Solidarity for Ever" was sung by the women's choir of the Wellington Trades Council. Notable trade union leaders attended, as did David Lange, the leader of the Labour Party.

Ernie Abbot's coffin was then taken from the stage and placed on a cream utility vehicle outside. Flanked by 19 mourners and followed by an estimated crowd of 5000, the funeral procession slowly made its way through silent streets.

Many unions stopped work for the day as a mark of respect and as a sign of outrage at the murder. The morning Wellington ferry was cancelled because of a stopwork meeting by the Seamen's Union.

In Auckland, about 500 people gathered for a memorial service in Waikaraka Park Cemetery in Onehunga. In chill winds, one minute's silence was observed. Other ceremonies took place in Rotorua, Christchurch and Dunedin.

In the wake of the bombing, the country was hit by a spate of bomb threats. At 7.25 am the next day, the Labourers' Union National Headquarters received a hoax call. At 8 am, the Christchurch Star received a call from an English-accented voice saying the Canterbury Trade Union Centre was going to be bombed. The Whakatu freezing works near Hastings and the Waitaki works near Dunedin both received bomb threats. All were evacuated and searched but no explosive devices found.

A few days later, a suitcase similar to the one used in the Wellington murder was discovered in the hallway of an empty store in Lake Rd, on Auckland's North Shore. It was blown up by explosive experts and discovered to be empty.

There was also a curious aftermath when on 11 April some union officials, including FOL vice-president Sonja Davies, went to have lunch in the Brunswick Arms Tavern in Willis St, Wellington. Towards the end of the meal, one of the waitresses alerted Miss Davies to a man who was staring at her. She said the man resembled the identikit picture of the bomber. The police were called but did not arrive before the man left.

One of the female union executives followed him as he walked down the street and entered a building. The union official waited outside at a bus stop until the man came out.

She followed him again. Every so often, he glanced behind him as if looking to see if he was being followed. She kept up with him through several streets, taking off her pink cardigan so as not to attract his attention. Finally, he went across the road, ducking between moving cars and disappeared in Dixon St.

Three minutes later, the police caught up with the union official, but by then it was too late. The man had gone.

It was believed that the only reason Abbot's dog Patch survived the blast was because he was so close to the ground. If anybody else had been in the foyer at the time, it was probable that, like Ernie Abbot, they too would have been killed.

A few weeks after the explosion, Patch went home with his new owner, a young woman from Wellington, the daughter of a woman who used to clean Ernie's room. She picked him up from the Karori veterinary surgery, where he had been convalescing. When last heard of, the dog was living in Taupo.

A tree was planted in Cobblestone Park opposite the Trades Hall in honour of the cheerful caretaker, and a commemorative seat was placed in the foyer of the hall. It was made by the Carpenters' Union out of rimu salvaged from the blast and became known as "Abbot's Rest".

It remains uncertain whether the bomb was left in the Wellington Trades Hall with the intention of murder or partial destruction of the building.

The man in charge of the hunt for the murderer, Detective Inspector Ted Lines, believed that murder was always intended because of the amount of explosive used. Police carried out tests from which they calculated that the bomb had contained three sticks of gelignite.

It is probable he did pick up the suitcase immediately. The man who planted the suitcase had used a one-hour timing device to ensure it did not go off when he was carrying it. That had elapsed by the time Ernie Abbot finally carried out the duties of his job and attended to the suitcase.

When his body was discovered, his hand was open as if he had flicked the catches to try to look inside the case. One leg was more severely damaged than the other, as if he had been kneeling beside the case when it had exploded.

The bomb had been designed by an evil and clever mind. Whether Abbot opened or lifted the suitcase, the mercury was tipped, the connection made, and that was the last he knew of it.

10. Chris Bush

Highway Robbery

Maramarua is a small rural settlement about 50km south-east of Auckland along State Highway 2 on the way to Thames. Work in the region is mainly provided by forestry and milling. The focal points of the community are the local school, the rugby ground and the Red Fox tavern.

In 1987, the tavern was much like any other footy and racing-mad pub in New Zealand. On the wall was a poster of rugby league legend Mal Meninga. Beside it was a picture of All Black captain David Kirk kissing the first rugby World Cup that the All Blacks had won that year. The lounge bar radio was continuously tuned to Radio Pacific, blaring the action from race meetings all around New Zealand.

As usual, Labour weekend promised to be one of the

busiest of the year, and Chris Bush, the publican, was looking forward to a break after it. He had worked himself almost to the point of exhaustion. His barman had left a fortnight earlier for a better-paid job and a secretarial worker had also left for family reasons. Bush had been putting in extra hours and effort to cover for them.

He was looking forward to a free trip to the Melbourne Cup that the brewery had awarded him for having low costs and a high turnover in the tavern. It was an appropriate acknowledgment. Bush was a keen racing fan and had interests in several horses.

He had been the manager of the Red Fox for five years and was a popular member of the local community, someone people could lean on when they were down on their luck. Sometimes, he would lend money to people in need. Some of his cash he never saw again but, easygoing by nature, he never seemed to mind too much.

He was born in Wellington on Mother's Day 1944 and brought up in Lower Hutt. He attended St Michael's Church near his home, which has since been turned into a school. He later went to St Bernard's Primary School and St Patrick's College in Silverstream, where he was an accomplished schoolboy rugby player.

At the age of 15, he contracted rheumatic fever, which largely ended his sporting days though he did later play a game on the wing for the Taita Rugby Club in Wellington. His love of sport never wavered and he enjoyed squash, golf and fishing.

He became an accountant when he left school and worked for a variety of firms for nine years before abandoning the humdrum world of accounting for the hotel trade. He first worked in pubs in Wellington, and then afterwards Palmerston North and Taupo, before coming north to Maramarua.

Chris had married his wife, Gay, in February 1968 so that by Labour Weekend 1987 they were not far away from celebrating their 20th wedding anniversary.

On the Friday night of Labour weekend, Chris and Gay Bush went to the tavern to celebrate a friend's 50th birthday. Mrs Bush left at 10.15 pm and returned to their home, which was just across the road. Half an hour later, her husband closed the hotel and stepped out into the chill night air.

Straightaway, he noticed there were two cars parked outside the hotel, blocking the exits. The people inside them didn't appear to be doing anything. With some trepidation, Bush approached the cars and spoke to the people inside.

The cars drove away into the night without incident, but the situation had spooked Bush enough for him to tell his wife about it when he got home.

She already knew what a tough business it could be running a hotel. Gay Bush recalled the time her husband had worked at Flanagan's in Wellington several years earlier. It seemed that hardly a night went by when he did not come home with a black eye.

Apart from the risk of violence from drunks, the amount of cash that hotels took across the bar could also make them vulnerable to armed robbery. They had discussed that possibility from time to time. Chris Bush had promised his wife that if a robbery took place he would not resist. He would just open the safe and let the robbers have it all.

The main reason the Bush family had decided to move to the rural area of Maramarua was to escape the violence and crime of the city.

On that Saturday, Bush worked at the tavern during the day, then popped across the road for dinner and a bath before going back to the pub for the evening shift. When his wife Gay said goodbye to him, she had no idea that her worst fears were about to be realised.

It was a busy night and a lot of money was taken over the bar, as the clock inched its way towards closing time. Last orders were taken, people finished their glasses and slowly the bar was cleared of people. The staff busied themselves with the clearing-up, looking forward to getting home to a good night's sleep.

When one of the bar staff was about to leave ahead of the others, Bush asked her to stay because he was cashing up and did not like to be left alone while he was counting the money. When he had finished and the money was safely locked away in the safe, Bush generously shouted his hard-working staff a drink.

Barman Bill Wilson and barmaids Sherryn Soppet and Stephanie Prisk were only too happy to linger a little longer and chat now that the hard work was done. The time was about 11.30 pm.

They did not hear a car pull up outside. Inside it were at least two men and possibly a third. It is possible that one or more of them had been in the tavern that night. If not, they had probably been there on a previous occasion, sipping their drinks as they sat in the corner taking everything in.

Two of the men got out of the car. The third, the driver, stayed behind. The leading man was about 1.68m tall and of medium build. He wore dark overalls and a balaclava was pulled down over his head, hiding all of his face except for his eyes. He was carrying a sawn-off, double-barrelled shotgun.

The other man was about 1.8m tall and solidly built. He also wore mechanic's overalls and had a balaclava pulled tightly down over his head. He was carrying a baseball bat.

The car may have been parked in the gravel car park outside the tavern but it is more likely the men chose to park by the side of the road so they could walk noiselessly across the paddocks towards the pub's back door.

They paused there and listened to the sounds coming from inside. They had deliberately timed it so all the patrons would have gone home. In fact, they had left it late, hoping that the publican would be alone, but through the door they could hear the bar staff chatting and laughing.

The two men looked at each other, nodded, then burst into the tavern through the unlocked door.

What the robbers had not allowed for was that Bush was

News Media Auckland

A police reconstruction of the two armed robbers
who killed Chris Bush.

seated just a couple of metres away from the back door, enjoying his drink.

Caught by surprise when they burst in, he reacted instinctively. No one but him knew exactly what his intentions were. It could simply have been a movement of genuine surprise. It could have been that seeing two armed men, he instinctively moved across to stand between the gunman and one of his barmaids.

The gunman was nervous and the last thing he expected was to find someone so close. He reacted instinctively; he raised the gun and fired.

The shotgun blast struck Bush in the left side of the chest. The pellets pierced his heart and lungs, killing him immediately. He died without having exchanged a single word with his killer.

As he hit the floor, one of the robbers shouted at the stunned bar staff, demanding to know who had the keys to the safe. When told they were on Bush, one of the barmaids, Stephanie Prisk, was forced to search through the pockets of his bloodstained clothes for the keys while the other two were ordered to lie on the floor.

"If you don't find the keys, someone else will get it," screamed one of the robbers.

From where she lay on the floor, Sherryn Soppet saw the gunman kick Bush's body. She watched with horror as Stephanie Prisk, having retrieved the keys from Bush's dead body, was dragged towards the manager's office.

The gunman kicked his way through two locked doors to get in. By now, Stephanie Prisk was hysterical. She couldn't hold the keys properly, and she couldn't get the safe open. So the gunman dragged her by her heels back to the lounge bar where his accomplice was menacing the others with his baseball bat.

All three staff were then tied to the bar rails as the gunmen struggled with the safe lock. They finally managed to break into it and inside were the weekend's takings in cash of about $20,000 and about another $5000 from the TAB.

The three bar staff were told not to move for eight minutes or they would "get the same treatment [as Bush]". The men left by the same door they had entered through.

The two women managed to free themselves from their bonds and release the barman. They then phoned relatives and a group of friends from a nearby football club. Unsure if the robbers were still lurking around, they asked them to come over and protect them.

But the robbers had gone, driving down the dark night roads either in the direction of Thames or westwards back towards Pokeno from where they could have gone north to Auckland or south towards Hamilton. The shooting late at night at the country hotel meant police had no chance to quickly seal off the area.

The next morning, a special police base was set up outside the tavern and a special telephone line was established for people wanting to pass on information. About 30 patrons of the tavern who had come forward were interviewed, but the police did not gain a great deal of information about the masked robbers.

They began to search for clues in the vicinity. Ground searches of roadside scrub, bush and culverts extended out to a radius of 10km around the tavern. Metal detectors were brought in to scan bush and paddocks behind the tavern in case the sawn-off, double-barrelled shotgun had been dumped there. The search fanned out to the possible escape routes the robbers had taken down side roads.

The one tangible link with the killers was the unusual pieces of rope used to truss up the staff during the robbery. Police believe the two men brought the rope with them especially for the job. The yellow nylon rope appeared to be a single strand unravelled from a rope of two or more strands, with a green and white thread running through the centre. Attempts were made to trace the manufacturer of the rope.

The police carried out an unusual reconstruction in a bid to elicit information and support. They dressed up mannequins identical to the killer and his associate and placed them in view outside the Red Fox tavern.

Shortly before the attack, two men had knocked on the bottle store window. One was a motorcyclist who stopped about 11 pm and asked for directions to the nearest petrol station. The motorcyclist was wearing a full-face helmet, and his small machine had a red petrol tank. The other drove a blue or grey-coloured Chrysler Valiant with a black vinyl roof. He had stopped only minutes later and spoken to the barman. It was possible they could have been innocent parties or they could have been casing the bar before the robbery.

As a result of the investigation, there were many arrests as police inquiries made major inroads into the local underworld, but none of them was directly connected to the murder of Chris Bush.

One man was charged with the quite separate theft of a motor vehicle. The police also broke up a heroin ring and captured two escaped prisoners who were on the run.

Horrified by the callousness of the crime, known members of the criminal underworld came forward and offered information to police.

When a habitual criminal, William Raymond Grigsby, was being questioned in regard to the killing, he realised somebody must have fingered him and he decided to get his revenge by weaving "a web of nonsense" that put the police on the wrong track. He claimed to have the proceeds of the robbery and named the murderers.

At first, the police gave him the benefit of the doubt and put him up in an Auckland hotel for a week where he watched videos and drank beer at their expense. In the end, 25 detectives and a helicopter were assigned to Grigsby's wild goose chase. Based on his information, armed police raided a house in Thames, smashing down the door and bursting in brandishing guns, much to the consternation of the owner who later complained, "I can understand that they want to catch the murderers but this was far too over the top. And they wrecked my house."

Finally, when interviewed on 12 December, Grigsby admitted to police that all his information over the previous week had been false and that he had never had the money stolen in the armed raid.

On 21 December, the 25-year-old Southland man was convicted in the Otahuhu District Court of attempting to obstruct justice by giving the police false information on three separate occasions. Grigsby was remanded to appear in the Invercargill District Court, where he was ultimately sentenced to 10 months' imprisonment.

Police received several anonymous letters from people claiming to know about the killers of Chris Bush. The Auckland Star received a note scrawled on the back of an envelope flap giving descriptions of a man and woman, their occupations, and the message: "Hope this may help Chris Bush."

The owners of the Red Fox, Hancock and Co Ltd, offered a $15,000 reward for information leading to the murderers. This was increased to $30,000 when the Hotel Association matched the offer.

Chris Bush's funeral was held on 29 October at the clubrooms of the Maramarua Rugby Football Club. As a mark of special respect, his body lay in state at the Mangatangi Marae beforehand. Many local residents chose to visit the body there, where they could speak freely to him. Bush was one of only three non-Maori to have been accorded this honour.

As the funeral went on, the Red Fox tavern remained closed until mid-afternoon out of respect. Amongst the close-knit Maramarua community that gathered to farewell the body and spirit of Chris Bush was his widow, Gay, and their two daughters, Jodie, aged 17, and Penny aged 15. They clung to each other for support during the half-hour Catholic service. An estimated 800 people packed into the clubrooms or stood silently outside in the light drizzle.

After the burial in the Maramarua Cemetery, a group of

Maori people went to the Red Fox tavern, where one of them, Rua Cooper, performed a Maori ceremony to lift the tapu. The staff had felt uneasy about working in the bar since the murder, and had asked for the ceremony to be done. They huddled together weeping as Cooper carried out their wishes.

Gay Bush regretted that she was never able to say goodbye to her husband's body on the night of the murder. By the time the local residents had taken the walk across the road to tell her the grim news, the police had already turned the tavern into a crime investigation scene. For several weeks, she could not bring herself to return to the bar.

But she decided she must confront her demons and also do something that would represent the spirit of her husband. So she organised a Christmas fashion parade in support of the local Hauraki Plains Rowing Club. About 180 locals packed into the tavern that night to see Chris Bush's daughter Jodie take part as a model and his other daughter Penny serve drinks.

For a time, Gay Bush took over as the publican at the tavern, but almost exactly a year after her husband's murder she and her two teenage daughters moved on to Taupo.

Before they left, they did experience a night to remember when the tavern seemed to be filled with her husband's easygoing spirit. It was the Saturday late in January 1988 when Chris Bush's horse Dark Lace won the $10,000 Norwood Metric Mile at the Counties Racing Club's meeting at nearby Pukekohe.

Before his death, Bush had bought a magnum of Moet champagne, with the promise that the top would come off it when the horse achieved its first win of the season. Later, Gay decided that she would crack open the champagne either when the horse won or the day the murderer of her husband was arrested.

If she had waited for an arrest, the bottle of champagne

would remain corked to this day. Without an informant or a confession, the police had little to connect them to the identity of the killers, who had melted away into the darkness of the night.

11. Maureen Ann McKinnel

Murder in Paradise

Arrowtown, in the middle of the South Island, used to be a big town in goldmining days. Back then, they had the odd murder or two, but when the miners left, the town became just another peaceful waystop for tourists visiting the beautiful and tranquil lakes of Central Otago. It was a place for families and old folk, where women could stroll at night without fear and house doors could be left unlocked.

But, ironically, at about 1.20 pm on the last day of 1987, Thursday 31 December, it was an amateur goldminer on holiday from Napier who made a gruesome discovery.

He was planning on panning for gold along the banks of the Arrow River but, standing at the roadside, he couldn't quite work out how to make his way down to the water's edge. As he looked straight down over the side of the bridge he saw the torso of a naked body, lying face down on the bank directly under the span of the bridge.

He immediately ran to the nearest house and raised the alarm.

The body was female and starting to blacken from decomposition. The police did not take long to identify it. A local resident, Maureen Ann McKinnel, had been reported missing since Boxing Day. Because of the state of the body, her immediate family was unable to make a positive identification and police used dental records to confirm her identity.

In life, Maureen had been a tall, 38-year-old blonde with a warm smile, laughing eyes and a gift for making people feel comfortable. She had managed the Marquise women's fashion store in Queenstown Mall since the previous April. Before that, she had spent several years working in Australia but had returned to New Zealand to be near her family. For the past three years, she had lived alone at her parents' holiday home at 3 Ritchie St, in Arrowtown. It was from there that she had disappeared.

The day before she died had been a happy one for her. It was Christmas Day. She had travelled from her house to her parents' home at Middlemarch, a country town about 60 kilometres west of Dunedin. She would have driven along picturesque country roads arriving at about 11.30 am.

She spent the whole day there with her family, which included her sisters and their families. It was a normal Christmas Day, full of presents, food and laughter. Then she set off for home at about 7 pm in her mustard-orange Honda Civic.

She would have felt relaxed after a special day with her family driving home through idyllic countryside that was enhanced at that hour of the day by the diffuse light of the setting sun.

Maybe she would have preferred to stay a few more days with her parents but, as the manager of a retail shop, Boxing Day was one of the busiest days of the year. She arrived for work at the Marquise fashion shop at about 10 am on that day and left again at 6 pm, driving home through Frankton, where she stopped to buy vegetables for dinner that evening. On the way home, she also paid a visit to a local Arrowtown shop.

That evening from about 7.30 pm until 11 pm, she entertained a male friend for dinner. That was the last time she was seen alive.

What happened then?

At 11.55 pm that night, a witness saw a Honda Civic similar to the one owned by Maureen being driven west along Kent St, which runs parallel to Ritchie St. Despite appeals from the police, the driver of this car never came forward.

About 20 minutes later, at 15 minutes past midnight, a shiftworker was driving to Queenstown past Maureen's house in Ritchie St and noticed that the lights were still on and the curtains drawn.

Later that morning, at about 8 am, neighbours noticed that the Honda Civic was parked unusually in the carport. The curtains of the house were drawn and the windows shut. The cat was waiting outside the door.

The same shift worker who had passed the house at midnight passed the house again at noon that day on his way home. He thought it strange that the curtains were still drawn.

That day was a Sunday and she had been expected in for work at the boutique. When she did not turn up for work, the alarm was raised. Police broke into her home. In the bedroom they found signs of a struggle. Some furniture had been dislodged and the bedclothes were in disarray. A murder inquiry was immediately launched.

The post mortem examination conducted in Invercargill revealed Maureen's killer had strangled her with his bare hands. As a result, she had died of asphyxiation. There were bruises and abrasions on her body which were consistent with her having put up a struggle. Because of the time that had elapsed in finding the body and its state of decomposition, evidence of sexual assault could not be established.

A team of more than 20 detectives from Invercargill, Dunedin, Alexandra and Queenstown, assisted by two DSIR scientists and forensic experts from Wellington, set out to find the killer. More police were added from Otago and Southland and some Christchurch uniformed police in the area for New Year's Eve celebrations were soon seconded to the inquiry.

A close inspection was made of the interior of the house and items were taken away for examination. Part of the veranda of the house was removed from the scene by forensic scientists. The investigative team had found "footprints and things" on it. The drains were also inspected to see if they might yield any clues.

Pictures of the area where Maureen's body was found were taken from a helicopter and the road closed for five hours while police searched the vicinity for clues.

From the start, police suspected that Maureen's Honda Civic hatchback, registration number IP6204, had been used to transport her body. When initial tests failed to reveal any fingerprints, they utilised a new technique known as the "superglue" process.

The Honda Civic and some bedroom furniture were sealed in a container with 600ml of the superglue solvent that reacted with air. When released into the atmosphere, the solvent settled on surfaces and identified parts of the car which had been touched by skin. The white film would clearly reveal any fingerprints on the surface material.

Because of the poisonous nature of the fumes emitted, the process had to be carried out inside a freight container. Anyone who was not clothed in protective equipment was at risk from the fumes, so the area had to be evacuated for about 30 minutes.

Timing was critical to opening the container. If the items were confined too long, a white mass could form on them, spoiling the quality of any prints that developed.

When the container was opened, the results were not as good as expected. The small glue pots were topped up and the container closed for another attempt, but when it was opened a second time, no useable evidence was produced that led to the identity of the murderer.

The car had almost certainly been used by the murderer because the keys were missing. The key ring which contained both car and house keys was a gold metallic ring with a tag which had writing on it. The police would not release details of what the writing said.

Three police divers from Wellington began a search for the keys at the Arrowtown River Bridge site where the body had been found. At the same time, soldiers from Burnham army camp used metal detectors along the entire road verge from the murder scene to where the body was dumped.

Also missing from Maureen's home were a cotton jewellery holder and a ring she was wearing when she was last seen alive. It had three oval garnets mounted on a gold band and it was valued at around $300. It was doubtful that theft was the motive for removing them. So why had the murderer taken them?

In 1993, a television programme about the ring prompted a woman to come forward with a ring, believed to be Maureen's, which the woman's mother had found in Lake Wakatipu.

At the time, police were also anxious to trace the owner of a green Mercedes-Benz which had been seen parked outside the Ritchie St house several times in the preceding months, but the owner never came forward.

One major problem the police faced was that Arrowtown was swelled by summer holidaymakers. There were an additional 2000 people staying at the local camping ground alone who were potential witnesses or suspects. The male friend who had dined with Maureen on the evening of Boxing Day was ruled out of the inquiry.

The murderer may have been a prowler. More than 10 Arrowtown women came forward with reports of prowlers over the previous few months, three of which had occurred since Maureen was strangled on Boxing Day.

On 28 December, a 23-year-old woman woke to find a man standing in the doorway of her bedroom. He was about six feet tall with broad shoulders. He was wearing a jacket. The woman was too frightened to move. She remained motionless and watched the man move around the house before he left without taking anything.

At another house, a man was reported to have stumbled through an unlocked sliding door. Perhaps drunk, he left without any further incident.

On another occasion, an elderly woman heard someone testing the lock on the back door of her home just before midnight.

The previous year, Maureen had also reported a prowler. In February 1987, a man walked into her bedroom but left after she threw a lamp at him.

Police were also eager to hear from a mystery person she was heard talking to the week before she was killed. A relative was staying with Maureen at the Ritchie St house on 19 December. That night, Maureen had gone out to an end of year party for local retailers in Arrowtown. She drove home alone, arriving just after midnight. As she was outside, the relative overheard Maureen holding a "murmured" conversation with the mystery person, though the relative was unable to tell if the voice was male or female.

A memorial service was held for Maureen McKinnel in Queenstown's St Andrew Presbyterian Church on 11 January 1988. The church was filled with many Queenstown businesspeople, friends and relatives including her parents, Matt and Mavis McKinnel. The head of the inquiry, Detective Inspector John Rattray, and several other police officers were also in attendance.

Former Queenstown retailer Stuart Graham, who employed Maureen for two years in his menswear store, gave an oration saying she had "touched the hearts of many people of all ages".

A Maureen McKinnel Memorial Fund was subsequently established to help finance a Queenstown women's crisis team intended to support the rehabilitation of women who had suffered incest, rape and abuse.

The police conducted a reconstruction of what they believed happened on the bridge, using Maureen's mustard-orange hatchback. A Queenstown locksmith was brought to Arrowtown to start the car. Then it was driven to the bridge and parked in several different places as police tried to picture how her body might have been dumped over the bridge.

The car was parked first on the gravel verge before the bridge, then on the bridge above where the body was found and finally closer to the rail, with the passenger door open. Each scenario was photographed.

Police requested information from local farmers who kept weather records. They hoped these would help the forensic scientists to establish when the body had been thrown off the bridge.

The local rubbish dump at Tucker's beach beside the Shotover River was turned over in the search for clues. The dump was placed under 24-hour guard for the duration of the search, but despite a painstaking hunt through decaying rubbish, nothing of interest was found.

There was a bizarre development in the case when clothing was found buried in Dansey Pass, north of Otago. The men's and women's clothing was found in good condition in a shallow hole on 14 January by people who camped by the Maraewhenua River. The clothing, which consisted of a woman's size 12 fawn trousers, a silk blouse, a blue bra and white singlet, a man's handkerchief, trousers and leather belt, a black plastic comb and a blue-striped, medium-sized shirt, was dug up by a dog. The people who discovered it handed it to Oamaru police who notified the McKinnel homicide team.

Subsequently, a somewhat embarrassed couple came forward to claim the clothing. They had been skinny-dipping in the river when somebody had come along, stolen their clothes and buried them. Not only were the skinny-dippers forced to drive home shivering in the nude but the prank had also implicated them in a murder inquiry.

The police continued to track down Maureen's contacts in the hope that they would come across the murderer.

One man they sought was an athletically built man of about 40 who was seen hugging Maureen at her work one day in early December. Just before Christmas, Maureen was seen talking to a well-dressed man in his mid-40s in the Marquise fashion shop. He was carrying a briefcase, looked like a businessman and was believed to be from Invercargill.

Another mystery man was seen at the Ritchie St house on Christmas Eve. Police were also seeking a goldminer seen under a large cottonwood tree 300 metres upstream from the Arrow River Bridge on 27 or 28 December and a Maori woman seen at the bridge on 30 December, the day before Maureen's body was found.

Police also hoped to track the killer by the vehicle he might have been driving and were anxious to locate a white-coloured car, possibly an early model Toyota Corolla, which was seen by a bus driver parked on the wrong side of the Arrow River Bridge between 1 am and 1.10 am on Sunday 27 December. They were also seeking a Toyota Landcruiser-type four-wheel-drive vehicle seen in Ritchie St on 27 or 28 December. It was light fawn or beige with a spare tyre mounted on the back.

In the small, close-knit Arrowtown community, the names of some of the men police were treating as suspects soon became common knowledge as police questioned friends and workmates.

One man who came under suspicion was quoted as

saying to the Dominion Sunday Times that he hoped the police would make an arrest soon, so that he would not have to suffer further public attention. He was feeling the pressure because the night Maureen was killed he was at home alone watching television – which does not constitute an alibi.

The suspect was getting fed up with getting strange looks in the street and being snubbed by people he knew. Gradually, the police inquiry narrowed the list of suspects down to just two men.

One was a Wellington man who had tried to strangle his girlfriend the year before. He had been on holiday in the area at the time of the murder. A pubic hair had been found on the man. Forensic tests have not proven it to be Miss McKinnel's but it is hoped that in the future new forms of scientific testing might prove that to be the case.

The other suspect was an Australian. He had lived in Queenstown for about five years but returned to Australia soon after the inquiry started because of "personal circumstances". He was known to have lied to detectives during interviews.

Only the murderer, who is perhaps one of these two men, knows what really happened to Maureen McKinnel on what should have been for her a relaxing and enjoyable Boxing Day night. After hosting a meal for her male friend that evening, she saw him off and secured the door. Then she went to bed.

Somehow, the murderer got into the house. Did he force his way in or was he someone who was known to her? Did she let him in?

Either way, he became an intruder. Though the decomposition of the body made it impossible to prove that she had been sexually assaulted, the fact that her body was found naked strongly implies that was the case.

She was either already in the bedroom or forced into the bedroom. She was an independent and spirited woman and when the intruder made advances towards her, she resisted.

The state of the bedroom told the story of a violent and desperate struggle. Almost a year before, she had repulsed an intruder by throwing a lamp at him but this man was stronger and more determined.

He forced her onto the bed, punching and hitting her. Possibly he raped her. What is certain is that at some point his strong hands wrapped around her neck and strangled her.

Whether she died at that point is not certain. She might have remained alive, breathless but not yet dead.

At this point, the murderer didn't panic. He must have sat down and thought the situation through. He had a dead body on his hands. If he left it there it could incriminate him, especially if his semen was still inside her. He had to delay the police investigation by removing the body from the scene.

But why did the murderer use the victim's car? Either he had great nerve or he did not have his own car there.

Under cover of darkness, he carried the body into the Honda Civic and drove probably down Adamson Drive and along Centennial Avenue towards the Arrow River Bridge. Or he might have taken one of the back roads – either along Lake Hayes Rd or along the gravel of McDonnell Rd.

Two people were out walking along Kent St close to the McKinnel house late on that Boxing night. At about 11.55 pm, they saw an orange Honda Civic being driven along the road by a man. Was Maureen's naked body slumped in the back seat?

It is possible that the murderer was not a local and did not know where to dump the body. Though the body was concealed well enough not to be found for several days, he could still have selected a more secret place than under the Arrow River Bridge.

And it was lucky he was not caught that night as it is a busy stretch of road in the tourist season. He pulled up close to the bridge, dragged her body up onto the railing, then toppled it over the side.

If Maureen were dead at this point, the body would have somersaulted lifelessly downwards. If she was still alive, it is possible the sudden rush of the chill night air might have partially revived her so that she was aware of falling, but when she hit the bottom the fall would probably have killed her.

Only the killer knows if he intended her to fall where she did. He might have cunningly intended her to fall in such a way that she landed almost obscured under the arches of the bridge. But he might also have intended her to fall into the water.

Then he got back in the car and returned it to the house where he had committed the murder. Why?

Surely if he had originally arrived at the McKinnel house on foot, he would have abandoned the car elsewhere. That implied he was either living close to the Ritchie St house or his car was parked nearby.

One thing is certain. He took Maureen McKinnel's car keys to hinder the investigation. Later, he disposed of them somewhere they have never been found.

In January 1989, on a trailer for a television current affairs programme, one of the officers still working on the case, Detective Jock Jensen, was quoted as saying, "We know who did it and he knows we know he did it."

So far that man has not come to trial because presumably the police do not have the evidence to prove it. If he is the murderer, only a handful of police officers are privy to the information which leads to him. The only other person who would have that information is the murderer himself.

12. Martin Owen Reid

The Secret Worlds of Martin Reid

Martin Reid was the sort of man who when he gazed up at the stars at night saw his own reflection. Yet his ambitions were bigger than his deeds and he ultimately died a lonely death. Worse, for several hours, no one even noticed.

His favourite book was said to be "Greed". It recounted the tale of New Zealand's most notorious drug dealer, Terry Clark, his associate Christopher Martin Johnstone and others involved in the Mr Asia Syndicate. Clark was the sort of person Reid looked up to. Clark had plenty of money, plenty of women, he thumbed his nose at the law, he travelled the world and he killed anyone who got in his way, even his closest associate, Christopher Martin Johnstone.

From the outside, it looked a glamorous life, but the criminal's lot is not a happy one. Failure is inevitable and no matter how much money he has he never really enjoys it. Nor did Martin Reid really have what it takes to be a ruthless criminal, because according to those who knew him best he was a generous guy at heart.

But Reid played the role of a big-time drug dealer, driving around in a big, white Chevrolet Camaro sports car. On 31 May 1988, several motorists noticed that distinctive car parked by the Garry River near Oxford about 70km north-west of Christchurch. The doors of the car were open and they could see a man lying on the ground, apparently working underneath the car.

When one local resident had driven past the car several times with the doors still open and the man on the ground had not changed position, the driver decided to investigate. Only then did he discover the man was dead. It was Martin Reid. He had been killed with a single shot to the head. There were injuries to his head consistent with his having being struck before he was shot.

Police found a sawn-off .22 rifle near the body. Scattered nearby were cannabis bullets. A shortened baseball bat was found in the car.

As the body was found at 5 pm in the afternoon and winter darkness was drawing in, the body was left in place overnight under police guard to allow for a more detailed examination of the scene the following day.

That night, the police set up roadblocks near the river, stopping passing motorists to ask them if they had noticed any suspicious activities in the area.

The next day, police made a more detailed examination of the scene. They found broken vegetation marks in the undergrowth nearby and soil near the car that pointed to a struggle having taken place before Reid's death. Forensic tests suggested that the weapon found at the scene had been used to kill Reid. A single Winchester shell that had been fired from the weapon was recovered.

For 19 days, the police searched the riverbed which had been the scene of the crime. A shingle riverbed is not an easy place in which to find clues. Army personnel assisted with the removal of scrub. A large area around where the Camaro had been parked was swept by metal detectors.

The police discovered two lots of .22 ammunition that had been recently discharged in the area. None of the spent shells had come from the cut-down rifle found at the scene, but the police sought to find out who had fired them, so they could eliminate the shells from the inquiry.

About 30 spent shells bearing the letter H on their bases, indicating the Winchester brand, were found directly opposite the car, 30m to 40m towards the Garry River. They were on a raised shingle area which becomes an island when the river is swollen.

Detectives began to investigate Reid's unusual lifestyle. Officially, he described himself as a self-employed, second-hand bicycle dealer. He ran his business from a house in Kaiwara St, Hoon Hay, where he lived with a woman neighbours knew as Mrs Vanessa Reid.

The couple had lived in the house, which was rented from a policeman, for about 18 months. Neighbours described them as a quiet couple who kept to themselves, though people often came to the house, especially at weekends, when Reid presumably sold his bicycles.

In fact, Reid was not married to Vanessa – she was his fiancée and he did a lot more than just sell bicycles. There was a lot more to Reid than met the eye and like most criminals, the whole amazing story only came out after he died.

Reid was born on 2 August 1960. He never knew who his parents were and was adopted out to become the only child of otherwise childless parents. At school, he suffered in the classroom but excelled at sport. He was in his high school rugby team from an early age and was also a champion sprinter. But he started to go off the rails, falling in with a bad crowd. After school he sometimes went to a nearby shopping mall to look for fights and other "action". He first fell foul of the law in 1974 when he was convicted of a burglary and fined $20.

Reid was always popular with his female classmates. It was a trait that was to continue throughout his life.

When he left school aged 16, he drifted from job to job, including working for the local council, at a car assembly plant and in a timber mill. During that time, he also received convictions for assault, burglary and weapons and firearms offences.

He had also worked as a driver for a Christchurch removal firm, a job which took him throughout New Zealand. In the 1980s, he started making trips to Sydney and it was here, apparently, that he first dabbled in hard drugs. According to one woman, who said she lived with him at the time, he also operated there as a male prostitute. Even if that was the case, he did not get into any trouble with the authorities in Australia.

In 1984, he returned to Christchurch with a woman called Linda but by 1988 his love life had got even more complicated, a fact that did not come out until after his death when the tangled web of affections was fully revealed.

Two death notices appeared in a local paper following his murder. In one Reid was the "much loved partner and life companion of Vanessa". Directly underneath, a notice announced he was the "dearly beloved fiancée of Lisa".

Reid had been living with two different women in Christchurch and, despite the addresses being just a few kilometres apart, neither knew the other one existed. Early in May, Reid had taken one of them, Lisa, on holiday to Queenstown, where he bought her an engagement ring. To complicate matters, he also had a son, Ben, aged about 3 years, by another woman. He had kept in close contact with his son.

In a bid to please both his partners, Reid juggled possessions between the two houses he maintained in Kaiwara St, Hoon Hay, and Jervois St, New Brighton. He wove an intricate web to maintain his complicated lifestyle, telling his fiancées he was a shift worker. It was perhaps even more complicated, because police believed he probably had other girlfriends as well.

After Reid's death, in order to accurately track his movements, the police arranged for the two women to meet at the police station in what was described as "a constructive meeting".

Reid maintained the lavish lifestyle of an American gangster, running two houses and one flashy car. When the police checked Reid's bank statements, they found he had been withdrawing around $2000 in cash a week.

Reid financed his lifestyle not with big deals but with borrowing. When he died, he was about $40,000 in debt. He owed $12,000 on the Camaro, he still owed $7000 on a car he had since sold (the new purchaser got a shock when he found out there was still money outstanding on it) and he owed his mother $10,500. He also owed $15,000 to a local businessman who had lent him the money on the basis that Reid had a big drug deal coming up from which he would be paid back.

Yet big-spending Martin Reid had blown most of the money. When he died, he was down to his last $3 and, a few days earlier, he had sold his tools for $200 to raise needed cash.

One of the greatest difficulties of the investigation was that Reid had concocted a Walter Mitty-type fantasy world around himself. His life was a tissue of lies and illusion, with different lies being told to different people.

Reid kept a phone book with all the names and telephone numbers written in code. Reid had used the coding system from "Greed", which had pride of place beside his bed. It was both his bible and his fantasy. Experts were brought in to crack the code in Reid's address book, but when they could not, they began to believe that the book was itself an elaborate fiction.

As a result of the intense investigation into Reid's death,

the police were able to identify the pecking order of criminals and the flow of drugs within the Christchurch underworld, but there was no trace of the cocaine ring Reid always claimed he was a part of. The police did not find out who were the two Christchurch lawyers that Reid said were the ringleaders, nor could they locate any of the other members of the syndicate.

In his fantasy world, Reid was a big wheeler-dealer. In reality, he was a petty thief and con man, living his life by a succession of failures that others inevitably inherited.

In the last few days before his death, Reid had confided to friends that he was involved in a big drug deal. The deal was due to be made on either Monday 30 May or the next day. Something major had definitely been planned because as those dates approached Reid started getting edgy.

Drug dealers and other criminals were in the habit of leaving the city environs of Christchurch for the isolated countryside to do deals. The police investigation was assisted by Reid's flamboyance in driving a big American car – probably not a wise type of vehicle for a supposed drug dealer to drive as it made him extremely visible and easy for the police to track.

Police knew from definite sightings of Reid's white Camaro that he was in Oxford the Sunday before his death. He arrived at about noon and was there for several hours.

They also believe that during the following week he made a number of trips to the Oxford area.

On Tuesday 31 May, Reid arrived at the house he shared with fiancée number 2, Vanessa, in the early hours of the morning, and left a pistol there. He said he would return for it later. He then went to a bathhouse in Montreal St called Cat Ballou for a massage.

Afterwards, he went back to Vanessa's house and collected the pistol. She talked to him and noticed he was edgy. Then at 2.45 am he went to the house he shared with fiancée number 1, Lisa. He talked nervously to her and told her he had given a cocaine dealer some samples and was waiting for the results.

He also told her the criminal's lament, repeated by others many times before and since, that this was supposed to be his last deal. Unfortunately for him, he was right, but not in the way he expected. That he was in fear of his life, however, was undoubtedly true, as can be judged by the hand-written note he left Lisa that night:

Well sweetie,

If you are reading this, things must be going to go awfully wrong for me when I leave to finish the deal in an hour.

So – I love you more than anyone or anything before.

God I hope you never have to read this letter. I hope I'm home soon to tear it up and we can have that wonderful life together I've planned for us both.

So here's hoping
All my love for always
Marty

He went out again at 4 am but returned three-quarters of an hour later saying all had gone well. The drugs had been delivered and the money taken to the lawyer's house. He seemed relieved.

But was there something more required to conclude the deal? The next morning at 10.15 am, Reid set out to meet someone. He drove along Waimairi Rd, along the Tram Rd heading towards Oxford and then through Main St, Oxford. His route took him through the Ashley Gorge towards the Garry River Bridge. His distinctive car was sighted at several points along the way.

At 11.29 am, he stopped and talked to two Telecom linemen who were working at the side of the road. He asked them if they had seen a red Commodore or a blue station wagon.

Twenty minutes later, his car was seen driving across the Garry River Bridge in the direction of Loburn. Five minutes later, his car was seen coming back the other way, as if he was searching for the people he was supposed to meet.

At 12.15 pm, the Camaro was seen parked at the intersection of Apiaries and Mountainview Roads. Between 12.30 pm and 1 pm, four witnesses saw the car parked in the Garry riverbed.

The car was there for many hours before the curious motorist investigated at about 4 pm and made his gruesome discovery.

A teal-blue Austin Westminster, or a similar model, was seen parked near Reid's car in the riverbed about 3.15 pm. The same car was observed parked at the intersection of Birchill and Baird Roads about 1km away about two and a half hours earlier at 12.50 pm that afternoon. Two people were sitting inside it. Earlier it had also been seen parked in nearby No 1 Road.

Several teal-blue Austin Westminsters were checked by the police and discounted from the inquiry, but the one they were seeking was never found.

An old Morris Oxford or Wolseley was seen parked behind Reid's car. It was traced to a man known to be involved in the local drug scene. He immediately became a suspect.

When a criminal murders a criminal, it is so much harder to gain a conviction. The code of silence rules and the suspects interviewed often become like the three monkeys who saw nothing, heard nothing and are definitely saying nothing.

Reid also had enemies. On 25 May, six days before Reid died, Christchurch police received a strange phone call. The speaker called himself Peter (this was almost certainly not his real name). He told the police that Reid was a dealer and offered to set him up. The officer taking the call tried to get a dialogue going with the caller. Finally "Peter" hung up with the chilling words, "If you don't do anything, I will deal with it in my own way."

Police believed that, because of the fears Reid had for his life, when he went to the Garry River meeting he might have had a back-up watching from a distance.

They appealed for that person to come forward and also offered promises of immunity to members of the criminal fraternity who had information about the murder but who had not been a principal offender. Four people took up the offer and provided information, though none was particularly valuable.

The police had several suspects. One was a man who had a cannabis plot 500m from where Reid was killed. Reid bought cannabis from the man to sell and it was rumoured the man had asked Reid to be involved in any cocaine deals Reid was setting up. Reid had told the man he would have 14 grams of cocaine at the end of May.

But police found no evidence against the suspect to implicate him in the murder. He also had the perfect alibi – he was in court at the time Reid died.

Another man who came under suspicion was well known to the police as a drug dealer. An associate of his, who was living in the same house at the time, was an experienced standover man.

There is no doubt that Reid was the architect of his own death. He lived a lifestyle that attracted violence without having the necessary courage to face up to it or dispense it. He went to the Garry River for a reason that remains vague to this day.

One theory was that it was suicide. He knew his debts were spiralling out of control. His creditors were closing in on him, as were members of the criminal underworld to whom he had promised deals but which he couldn't deliver. He had sawn down the gun so that his finger could easily reach the trigger, he had said goodbye to those he claimed to love and then he went to the forest to end his own life.

But before he pulled the trigger, as part of the image he

had painted of himself, he decided to fake his own death and make it look like a "hit". Isn't that the way a big man in the criminal world is supposed to go out? He made it look as if a struggle had taken place first, as if he had fought to the last. Then he had scattered cannabis bullets around the area to make it seem as if a major drug deal had gone wrong. It would have looked better if he had had cocaine, but he alone knew the truth – that behind all the empty boasts he didn't have any. Having constructed his own epitaph, he then shot himself.

That scenario is possible, but seems unlikely.

Another theory was that Reid shot himself by accident. On inspection, the rifle he had brought with him proved to have a light trigger. He could have been brandishing it around, acting out his own toughness before the deal, and in his nervousness shot himself. Also unlikely.

Another theory was that Reid was getting too big for his boots and needed to be put in his place. He knew this was on the cards, which was why he brought the gun. Then the people he was meeting had spotted the gun in the car or they had dispossessed him of it. They had held it to his head as a form of threat, unaware of the hair trigger. When Reid had nervously pushed the gun away, it had gone off.

But the evidence points more clearly towards murder.

On 30 May, when Reid visited his 3-year-old son, he seemed to be aware that this might be the last time he saw him. There was something of a farewell about the visit and there were tears in his eyes when he hugged him.

Back at his Jervois Rd home, Reid removed his rings and the Union Jack badge he liked to wear, and put them on top of the television set.

A week before, on 23 May, Reid had either bought or borrowed a .22 rifle from a friend. He said he was going rabbit shooting. He had also borrowed three boxes of Winchester ammunition, each containing 50 rounds.

It was probable that at least two other men were present beside the Garry River that day. Three empty beer cans were found at the scene. One of them was inside the car and the other two outside. Cigarettes had also been smoked and the butts left there.

It seemed from them that whatever meeting had taken place had started in a friendly manner. The central theme was almost certainly drugs. Reid might have been collecting his share of the proceeds from the big drug deal he claimed to have pulled off. He might have been delivering drugs in exchange for cash. He might have been ripped off by a standover man or fingered for something else entirely. By the nature of the life he lived, there were just too many possibilities why he was killed.

One theory is that Reid promised to deliver a large amount of cocaine, but intended to steal the money from those he was supposed to be selling to. His deception was revealed to the purchasers when they discovered his gun in the car. They turned it on him and shot him where he was sitting in the driver's seat. They dragged him out and along the ground, at which point his shoes came off.

Then they pulled the car apart looking for drugs. They made a hole in the dashboard and slashed the seats, but there were no drugs.

Whatever actually took place, it seems certain that at some point the meeting degenerated into disagreement. An argument broke out, followed by a scuffle. Vegetation was damaged, a broken wristwatch, believed to have been Reid's, was found close by.

It is likely that at this point Reid tried to get hold of his weapon, which was within reach. The other men jumped on him and struck him. They got his own rifle from him and shot him with it. Then they drove off and left him there.

But they realised they had been in his car and left their fingerprints all over the scene. Maybe they were based nearby, because one of them was able to pick up an old tea towel and return to the scene, which still remained as they had left it. The doors of the Camaro were still slung open and Reid's body was still slumped on the ground. Luckily for them, none of the passersby had even realised he was dead.

They wiped their fingerprints from the gun and the car with the tea towel then, as a final insult, arrogantly tossed it onto Reid's body. Did the murderers also scatter cannabis bullets around his body to imply that he had been involved in a deal which was different to the one they had actually been conducting?

The word "help" was scrawled on the side of the car. Did Reid write it in the dust and grime with his finger after he had been left to die or had it been written earlier by someone making a joke about his dirty car?

The footprint of a commando-style boot was found at the scene, but its owner was never located. Also found were the tyre tracks of the Oxford or Wolseley car. The tyre tracks went right over those of the Camaro so the car probably belonged to the killers.

There was also the possibility that Reid's complicated love life took its toll or that someone to whom he had owed money had decided to cancel the debt in the most final manner.

When the body of Martin Reid was laid to rest in Christchurch, the funeral service was held in secrecy. Afterwards, family members were tight-lipped about the details of the service, which was attended only by relatives and close friends.

Reid was adjudged bankrupt a month after his death. His assets were virtually nil while his debts totalled about $40,000. The white Camaro on which he still owed payments was repossessed.

Two years after the murder, on 28 June 1990, police received a call from someone who claimed to have been the back-up person at the river that day. The woman called herself Karen, and seemed to the policeman who took the call to be influenced by drugs or drink. She agreed to phone the following day but did not and police feared she had been threatened.

But then a few days later she phoned again. She named two men who were both in prison at the time as the murderers.

One of the men, who was serving a sentence in Paparua prison, had told a number of the other inmates during the previous few months that he had killed Reid. Detective Senior Sergeant Brian Pearce was quoted at the time as saying, "The information we have been given confirms our belief of this person's involvement, but the extent to which the man claims to have been involved in the killing is not consistent with the facts as we believe them to be."

The last time the woman phoned she said she was going overseas. Police had immediately mounted a special watch on departing passengers at Christchurch International Airport, but the woman was never seen or heard from again.

There was one last secret to come out of the many lives of Martin Reid. Only a few months before he died, Reid had tried to discover the identities of his birth parents through the Adult Adoption Information Act. He filled out the forms and put through an application but the forms came back declined.

When his real mother had put him out for adoption, she had put a stop on him ever finding out who she was. She never wanted to make contact with her son.

It took a murder inquiry to break down this barrier of silence. It turned out that Reid's father was born on the wrong side of the tracks. He had seduced Reid's mother, who was from a wealthy family, when they were both teenagers. She was 14 years old when she gave birth to Reid and quickly cut all ties with him.

His real father, the police discovered, was called Wayne Beri. Neither Beri nor Reid had any contact with each other over the years and were unaware of each other's existence. The police did not have any difficulty tracking down Wayne Beri. He was in prison. When they informed him of the relationship, at first he did not believe them until he was shown the copy of Reid's birth certificate.

In 1985, Auckland police had conducted an undercover operation which they had codenamed Operation Fruit and the biggest pip in the basket was Wayne Beri. They kept a round-the-clock check on him for 10 weeks, bugging his house, his cars and a motel that he stayed at in Christchurch. Finally he was arrested, along with others, and brought to trial, where he was convicted of importing heroin.

In sentencing Beri, Mr Justice Thorpe said he was the top man of his operation – one who was prepared to carry and use firearms to protect himself. He was sentenced to life imprisonment.

Without even knowing it, the boy who had illusions of becoming a drug overlord was himself the son of one.

He also had an extended family he didn't even know about. One of his cousins, Mark Beri, would have been a nephew of Wayne Beri. They would not have known it even if they had met and it was possible they did meet because Mark Beri, who died of cancer in 1993, was the chief suspect for the murder of Martin Reid.

Mark Beri had been a big man, 1.9 metres tall. Police believed he was part of a gang of five who were ripping off drug dealers at the time of Reid's death. Beri, with his intimidating presence, was the standover man for when things got out of hand.

An informer placed Beri at the murder scene, saying that at the time he was on a dangerous cocktail of drugs. However, the informer was himself a man involved in the drug world whom the police described as a con man loaded with cunning. While placing others at the scene, he conveniently made sure he had an alibi. The police believed the informer gave them information that could only have been known by somebody at the scene.

The accusation that his nephew might have killed his natural son was all water off a duck's back to Wayne Beri sitting in enforced idleness at Paremoremo maximum security prison. "You play with fire, you get burnt," was his succinct and unsympathetic response.

When the relationship between Reid and Wayne Beri was revealed, Mark Beri made a point of visiting his uncle in prison to tell him he was innocent of the crime. Ten days before he died of cancer, lying on his sick bed, he again phoned him, crying down the phone and declaring, "It's nothing to do with me, Wayne."

So did Mark Beri kill the man whom he didn't even realise was his blood relative? The answer is uncertain. There are only three things in life that are certain – death, taxes, and the fact that you can't rely on the word of a drug dealer.

Candle in a
Thunderstorm

Prostitution is supposedly the world's oldest profession. It is also the loneliest. For all her pretended intimacy, a prostitute never really makes contact with her clients. Whatever the physical nature of the act they perform together, there is always a distance between them. The gap is never closed by anything as tender as love. It is normally bridged only by money. And occasionally by murder.

Probably the most famous unsolved murders in history took place in the East End of London between 7 August and 10 November 1888. The man who killed seven prostitutes was never caught but was known by the pseudonym of Jack the Ripper.

Six of the women were killed after soliciting the murderer. The bodies were dissected and on one occasion half a human kidney was posted to the police.

Prostitutes are easy victims for murderers. Instead of shying away, by their very nature, with fluttering eyelashes and plastic smiles, they strut willingly forward into their own graves.

Like all big cities, Auckland has thriving red light areas. There are three basic ways prostitutes acquire their clients. Massage parlours usually offer genuine massages followed by "optional extras". Escort agencies will send an "escort" to a hotel room or to someone's house. These venues at least offer some security to the prostitute.

At the lowest end of the scale is the "streetwalker", who hangs around shop doorways in Auckland's red light areas such as Karangahape Rd (locally known as K Rd) at the top of Auckland's main street, Queen St, and Fort St, at the other end of Queen St, near the docks.

These women have little choice whom they go with. They wait impatiently, stamping their high heels on cold stone pavements, until a car pulls up and a window is wound down. Then after a quick discussion about price, she climbs into the car. Plain sex uncluttered by emotions then usually takes place in the car or amongst the greenery of one of Auckland's parks.

That which we are all taught is private and personal is willingly revealed and presented for use. The prostitute makes noises that imply a union but her mind has been turned off, her emotions have been placed in a numb limbo. She waits only for her "client" to satisfy his physical needs until the rental period on her body ends. The money she receives is likely to be spent within a day, then the following night she makes her lonely strut down the street again.

The prostitute is vulnerable to all that life might throw at her.

In 1989, a teenage prostitute, Leah Stevens, disappeared from K Rd. It was not until 1992 that her skeleton was found in a pine plantation at Muriwai Beach. In 1998, a 28-year-old Mangere man was arrested and charged with her murder. His trial was still pending as the book went to press.

In May 1993, Jane Furlong was another teenage prostitute trawling for business along K Rd. Her life had seemed to be going backward almost as soon as she was born. She was a life-long victim.

She was just four years old when her mother, Judith, split up with her father in 1979. Two years later, after struggling to pay off two mortgages, her mother put her children into the care of the Dingwall Trust, a child and family support service in Papatoetoe, South Auckland.

It was intended to be a short-term arrangement but it was another seven years before Jane returned to the home of her natural family. At the age of nine, she was put into a foster family. The foster mother already had two sons by a previous relationship and Jane did not feel she was well treated.

In a school project in 1991, she wrote, "I was at Dingwall for two years but then this family came to find themselves a daughter. I felt so proud when they wanted me to live with them. I thought to myself, "I'll show mum. I've got a new mother now." They were charming enough at first then my "new mother" changed. It was almost as though she didn't want me anymore, only the money she received for looking after me."

Jane wrote this at about the time when she was in Form 2 and the pupils had received their school reports. One of her foster brothers received C and D grades and attracted great praise from his mother. When Jane got straight A's, her foster mother appeared uninterested and said, "That's nice, dear."

"My feelings have never turned around so fast, from being proud to feeling lower than a snake's belly," Jane wrote of the incident.

After five years with the foster family, Jane chose to board at Whangarei Girls' High School. There she played up, probably as a cry for help, hoping that someone would give her a talking to and the opportunity to spill her heart out to them. No one did and her life began to spin further out of control.

She tried to demand even more attention by getting involved in Satanism and witchcraft. She also started drinking.

One brief bright spot in her life was a relationship with a boy who was a gothic punk. Their friendship was strong enough for him to write to her when he went to London in 1989.

She was stunned when he committed suicide on his twenty-first birthday. She later wrote, "There must be such a thing as a broken heart because the pain I felt was unbelievable. I miss him heaps. But these things happen and he is still in my heart and my memories."

In November 1990, she and two other girls were accused of stealing money at the boarding school. The matrons went through the girls' personal belongings searching for the money. They even looked through their personal diaries in search of evidence that they had committed the crime.

They found nothing and yet the whole matter left an indelible mark on Jane's fragile emotions. She felt violated. For her, the action of intruding into her personal matters had been akin to rape.

She decided to protest and fight back. That night, she and the other girls climbed down the fire escape and ran away.

Jane was intelligent, spirited and aware, yet in her short life she seemed to experience little family love which is the warm nest in which a child's abilities and emotions blossom. Nor was school of any help to her. She was too strong willed and rebellious to survive in a school system which prefers to condition the child to fit into what is an already imperfect society.

Jane's favourite books were "Rumble Fish" and "The Outsiders" by S.E. Hinton. Rebel books. She had enough spirit to be of some use to society, but she let herself down and nobody helped to pick her up when she was most vulnerable.

No ear was bent towards her voice, nobody saw her for what she was or extended a helping hand. She could only speak through her poems.

A single tear trickles down my face.
A solitary tear,
all alone.
Kinda like the way I feel,
all alone.
No one to wipe away
my single tear,
My solitary tear,
All alone.

The following poem was written in 1991, and probably indicates that as a child she was sexually abused:

The fear you have set inside me
will never fade away,
The memories that I often see
haunt me every day,
Like words to a song,
It's fixed in my head.
The night you raped me
And filled my life with dread.

Jane lasted about four months at Papatoetoe High School, then she went to the liberal Metropolitan College in Mt Eden, followed by Penrose High School.

In the fifth form at school, she wrote her autobiography. Her teacher awarded her the highest possible marks for it – 20 out of 20. It was written in narrative prose, yet read like an epic poem, a lament to a life that should have been, yet underneath the words you get the feeling that the petals of hope will always meet their autumn and be cruelly trodden underfoot. The last lines read:

"Where do I go from here?

I think everyone should have dreams and goals which they can work for, however high they may seem. My main ambition in life is to become a child psychologist. It's something I know I'll do well at and I'm willing to achieve my goal...
I feel better, now that my attitude has changed. I no longer want to die, I want to live and fulfil my every dream and hope. I want to make my mark in the world."

Jane spent less than a month at her last school, Penrose High. There she made friends with another wild child, Amanda Watt. They started wagging school together, then finally left altogether. "Life seemed so much more fun," Amanda said later. "We wanted to have some."

They left home but needed money. They didn't have jobs and were too young to receive unemployment benefits. Their parents would not sign the forms to allow them to get a youth allowance.

Then, one night, Jane came home with a bundle of cash. She said she had been hitchhiking and a man had picked her up. He had offered her cash to perform a sexual act. From that night on, the girls took to the streets regularly. They were just 15 years old.

The following year Jane became pregnant to her boyfriend, Danny. After the baby, Aidan, was born she went back to prostitution.

On 26 May 1993, she went to work as usual. Danny dropped her off on K Rd outside Rendells drapery store at about 8 pm. Her friend Amanda Watt was there too. Watt got into a car to "do a job". When she got back, Jane had gone.

When Danny returned later to pick Jane up she still had not returned. She was never seen again.

Jane, who was a woman physically, but inside was still a lonely girl, had just disappeared.

She had red eyes and her naturally brown hair was dyed black. She stood 1.55 metres tall and weighed about 43 kg. On one shoulder, she had a Grim Reaper tattoo. There was a tattoo on her left wrist which covered a C-shaped scar and on one hip she had a love heart which was about the size of a five cent piece.

She was wearing a black mini skirt, black lace top, ankle boots and a brown leather jacket with tassels. She was carrying a green army canvas bag containing make-up and clothing.

At first it was thought that she might have just chosen to disappear. She had disappeared once before. That time she was away only five days after staying at the house of a friend.

This time there were supposed sightings of her staying in Wellington with a former boyfriend, but he denied it.

There were no signs of her being alive. If she was alive, she would have surely inquired about her son or tried to contact her boyfriend, friends or family. She stopped getting pills from the person who was supplying her with drugs. No withdrawals had been made from her bank account.

But some items were missing from her flat as if she might have planned to disappear. They included things she would have needed for travel, such as T shirts, dresses, shoes and her toothbrush. Nearly all her underwear had gone.

Her relationship with her boyfriend was best described as "volatile". If she did just choose to disappear, it was because she had little reason to stay.

The Sunday two weeks before she disappeared was

Mother's Day. Despite the fraught relationship with her mother in the past, she made a Mother's Day card for her which read:

"Dear Mum,
I guess this card sums up exactly the way I feel. I
do love you and always will. I hope no matter
what I say or do you will always love me too. All
my love Jane."

Next day they had an argument and Jane moved out of her mother's Onehunga home. That's when she borrowed several hundred dollars from friends for the bond for a flat. Some believe she took the money to run away with.

On the day she disappeared, she had dropped in to see her foster father, who worked in central Auckland. It was the first time she had seen him in about a year. He said she seemed happy enough. She showed him pictures of her baby. If she was planning to leave, was this her way of saying goodbye?

Police had a number of suspects for her murder. One of them she had an outstanding rape complaint against and was scheduled to testify against him. She claimed he had picked her up and raped her instead of paying for sex. The man, a 40-year-old businessman was on an "Ugly Mugs" list of clients kept by the NZPC (New Zealand Prostitutes Collective). These were men prostitutes had found to be difficult and dangerous.

After her disappearance, the trial of the man in question went ahead without her and he was convicted of assaults on other Auckland prostitutes and sentenced to 16 years in jail.

On 12 January 1997, a skull was found below the cliff face at Musick Point, near Howick Beach in Auckland. At first there were suspicions that it might have been Jane's, but the dental records did not match.

If she had chosen to pack up and disappear, it is likely

News Media Auckland

Amanda Watt, fellow street-walker and best friend
of Jane Furlong.

that she would have left the country. She appears to have been too gregarious a character to remain invisible for long.

It is also possible that she chose to disappear, but with someone who later murdered her.

If she was murdered by a client, she would have suffered a lonely death, probably in a wild place such as a forest or in the back of a car. Her body would have been disposed of in some place where it would not be easily found.

She left behind a son who is being brought up by her boyfriend Danny's parents. When last heard of, Danny was himself serving time in prison.

As Jane Furlong hoped in the last words of her school autobiography, she made her mark on some of those she passed in the night. Quite literally in the case of her friend Amanda Watt. She has the initials JMF tattooed on her arm. She had the tattoo done to remind others to continue the search for her fellow prostitute and soulmate.

She described Jane as, "very rude, very intelligent and she's got this beautiful voice. Warm and feminine, but it can be real bitchy. She was such a bitch but the best friend you could ever have."

14. Norrie Triggs

Hell Hath No Fury Like a Woman Scorned

The last time anyone saw Norrie Triggs alive, he was snoring loudly. The 51-year-old computer programmer, who worked in the Public Trust Office in Wellington, rented a bedsit in a converted garage at 4 Sandhurst Way, Chartwell. At about 2 pm on Monday 7 February 1994, Waitangi weekend, his landlady, Margaret Galvin, was passing the window outside the flat when she saw him lying fast asleep on his bed.

Triggs had only intended to live in the flat for two

months, but had stayed for 18. Despite having been there for so long, his flat was full of boxes and suitcases, which he had never bothered to unpack in the meantime.

The next time his landlady saw him was the following morning at about 10 am when she glanced through the window of the flat and saw her lodger sitting on the floor leaning against an armchair. She was unsure if he was asleep or not, but she was concerned that he would be late for work, so she entered the flat to wake him. When she realised he was dead, she called the police.

They took photographs of the body, which was in an unusual position. He was sitting on the floor with the torso of his body propped up against the chair and his head hanging backward loosely over the arm of the chair. His legs were neatly crossed at the ankles.

At the time of death, he had been wearing a rust-coloured towelling robe and a pair of blue underpants. His white shirt was lying nearby. It had bloodstains on the collar. On the rail in the bathroom, the police found a bloodstained facecloth that had been draped over the rail as if it had been hung up to dry.

Bloodstains were also found on the pillow of his bed, on a copy of the "Evening Post" and also on a suitcase. Someone had made obvious attempts to clean them up.

From the preliminary investigation, it appeared that Triggs had died after a blow or blows to the head. It was uncertain if an instrument was used or a fist. When police examined the windows and doors of the bedsit, they found no signs of forced entry, implying that Triggs had known his assailant and willingly let him enter his room.

The investigation tracked back over Triggs' movements leading up to Waitangi weekend. On Wednesday 2 February, he had returned to Wellington after visiting his sister Judi Schwass in Napier and his friend Kerry Green in Waikanae.

Triggs was a creature of habit. He was known to be a prolific Lotto buyer, sometimes spending as much as $80 a week on cards. Though he had won many fourth and fifth division prizes, he had never had a big win. Detectives wanted to identify his regular Lotto outlet as a baseline for his other movements.

Triggs usually went out for a drink in the evenings. He had a regular routine every Saturday night, in which he would start drinking at the Old Bailey Tavern on Lambton Quay, work his way to the Loaded Hog in Bond St, then on to Arena nightclub on Wakefield St. He also often had a meal at the Rose and Crown at lunchtime. He usually wore a white shirt, black trousers and a tie to hotels.

When at the pubs, Triggs spoke to a few people he knew but otherwise kept very much to himself. Though he had been a regular at the Old Bailey for more than four years, when interviewed, the duty bar manager, Fiona Jopson, was surprised to learn that he worked at the Public Trust Office next door.

From their inquiries, the police established that Triggs was seen at the Loaded Hog pub between 5 pm and 9 pm on the Wednesday night and at Shed 5 on Thursday evening.

On Friday 4 February, he was seen at about 6 pm in Kirby's Candies and Lotto Shop, where he purchased computer printed Lotto numbers. Normally, when Triggs came into the shop to buy Lotto tickets he was alone but on this occasion he was accompanied by a woman.

At about 6.30 pm, a woman and a man believed to be Triggs were the first patrons of the evening to walk into the Dada Bar and Restaurant in Edwards St. The woman ordered a glass of wine for herself and a Coca Cola and cloves for her companion. Triggs was known to like cloves with his drinks.

On Saturday 5 February, there was a confirmed sighting of Triggs alone in the Opera Restaurant and Bar at 1 am. That night there were street fights in Blair St in the early hours of the morning. One theory was that Triggs could have inadvertently become involved in a street fight and taken a beating. Unaware that he was badly injured, he could have gone home where his haemorrhaging gradually grew worse, causing him to slip into a semi-conscious state.

He had got into bed and then woken up when he realised he was bleeding into his pillow. He got out of bed, trying to rouse himself, but then became weak and sank to the floor. Slowly the life had ebbed from him and that explained the unusual position in which he had been found.

There was also a possible sighting of Triggs in the afternoon of 5 February in the Crofton Downs car park alone in a green car (he drove a green Mitsubishi Sigma). Another sighting of Triggs was made by a patron who saw him enter the Lord Nelson alone. Triggs talked to a number of people he knew while he was there. He was well known to many patrons in that bar for his preference for drinking quadruple McCallums whiskeys with cloves.

As police made investigations into the background of the middle-aged bachelor, an unusual picture began to emerge of a man who had few deep relationships and many temporary ones. According to Mrs Galvin, in the 18 months he had been renting the flat at her house, he had seldom received visitors or phone calls.

"He was a lovely man, very charming, a rather old-fashioned sort of gentleman, tidy and clean and polite," was how an old friend described him. "However, he could be cutting with his tongue and tended to retort sarcastically if provoked." His sharp tongue made it plausible that he might have got into an argument on the street and suffered a beating.

As has been mentioned, police go through a victim's contacts to get leads on the murderer. When the police inspected Norrie Triggs' address book, they got a lot more than they had bargained for.

In his flat, they found a book with almost 1000 names in it. Some of the numbers went back to when Wellington still had five and six-digit telephone numbers. But the most surprising feature of the address book was that very few of the names beside the numbers were male. Far and away, the vast majority of them were female. It turned out that Triggs was something of a ladies' man.

Instead of being a loner as had been initially surmised, over the years Triggs had had numerous girlfriends and sometimes several at once. He possessed what could be best described as an "unusual rapport with women". It was discovered that Triggs went by the nickname "The Moth" because of his tendency to flit around the doorsteps of attractive women. The police estimated that Triggs might possibly have slept with 900 women over a period of about 30 years or, on average, a different woman every fortnight.

His best friend, Kerry Green, said that Triggs was an old-fashioned chauvinist whom women found courteous and charming. He said his mate Norrie was a "personal package of charm" when it came to women. "He really didn't excel in any area except charm. His eye contact with women was amazing. His eyes had a hypnotic effect."

Another friend, Alan Marsden, who used to hang out with Triggs in Napier in their youth, also attested to Triggs' amazing effect on women.

"Even back then he had difficulty in maintaining a relationship with just one woman. I remember he had two regular girlfriends for quite some time. One was a conservative, must be home by 10 pm type. The other was more outgoing and always ready for a party. Both were attractive and popular. But Norrie could never choose between them. More than once, Norrie would turn up at a party or other function with one of them and the other girl would also be there… I could never understand why the girls put up with his two-timing. But they did. He did seem to have some special hold over women – almost Svengali-like."

One of Triggs' former lovers also came forward to describe how he had a way of making a woman "feel like a woman". She was from Hastings and would only give her first name as Erin. She said she had ended her affair with Triggs more than 20 years ago, but he had still been one of her most gentle and caring friends.

"My children loved him, he got on well with my husband. There was no antagonism with Norrie. He had all the old-fashioned qualities, like opening a door for a lady. His manners were superb and yet he was a very modern man – witty conversation and very entertaining."

When the family heard about Triggs' murder, one of the daughters, who was then a university student, had locked herself away and created a sculpture in his memory. The wooden sculpture was an abstract cross with newspaper clippings attached to it.

"The concept represents a peaceful, gentle, loving man," Erin explained. "My children loved him and told me a few years ago I should have married Norrie. But that's wishful thinking – all the women that Norrie knew realised he wasn't the marrying kind."

Dozens more women came forward to talk about Triggs and they apparently did not have a bad thing to say about him. An unusually large number of unaccompanied middle-aged women turned up at his funeral.

Most of Triggs' relationships were based on sex. Many were one-night stands with women he picked up in bars. He did not appear to want, or have the ability to maintain, a long-lasting relationship with a woman.

The police contacted about 400 of the women listed in Triggs' address book. More than half of the telephone numbers were eliminated as no longer current or had been duplicated.

But not all of the women listed in the book were single. At first, the police suspected that one of Triggs' affairs with a married woman had prompted a jealous husband to take revenge. It is a scenario that has been repeated time and time again in the history of murder. Few passions are as strong as the blind emotion that demands revenge after betrayal.

But as the police systematically went through every name in the book, they eliminated the hundreds of potential jealous husbands and boyfriends until none was left.

So was a woman the murderer? That might explain why Triggs' body had been left in such a tidy state with legs neatly crossed. Who but a woman, unthinking and distraught, would instinctively hang up a bloodied facecloth as if she was going to wash her face with it the next morning?

Forensic tests on Triggs' body revealed that he had had sex with a woman just before he was beaten to death. Was that the same one who had murdered him or did she leave his bedsit, only for another woman to come in afterwards?

If he had been murdered by a woman he had had sex with, perhaps they did not both interpret the act in the same way. For Triggs, it may have been merely a mechanical action he had repeated several thousand times before with several hundred women. Though he appeared to treat every woman with the same olde worlde courtesy, were the faces becoming a blur to him?

The woman lying beside him might have felt differently. If she was middle-aged, she was probably aware that these days she turned fewer heads than she used to. Instead, men were glancing at the bodies of women half her age.

She might have had a yearning inside her that she felt was being fulfilled by this man who lay beside her. His good manners and charm towards her seemed to tell her that he cared about her as deeply as she cared about him. She might have lain beside him with that most powerful and yet that most vulnerable of all emotions – love. She might have communicated that love to him somehow.

Then how did Triggs react? Did he parry her clumsy thrust with the charm for which he was well known or, perhaps tired, his guard let down by sexual fulfilment, did he let drop some unguarded comment, did his sharp tongue cut with the edge of cold steel straight into the beating heart of the woman beside him?

And did that emotion she had felt suddenly implode into a deep blackness inside her, calling up not only this but all former rejections until she was blinded with emotion and operating without thought, her only instinct was to physically attack him.

Perhaps he was lying on the pillow unaware of the effect his remark had had. His body was relaxed and unprepared.

Because he was lying down and in order to strike him with her fist or an object that she might have snatched up, the woman had to raise herself. She struck using her whole body. Then she struck him again and again until her anger was spent.

Then she drew back, probably crying at her own grief, until she realised he was not moving. The blows had proved fatal, one of them causing blood to leak into his brain.

Suddenly, the woman realised what she had done and the female instinct to soothe and repair rose within her. She tried to put it right. She tried to revive him. She fetched a facecloth from the bathroom. Like tending a child with a cut, she hoped that if she wiped away the blood everything would be all right.

She tried to tidy up, but it was hopeless. Finally, in one last act of respect and regret, she tidied his body so that in death he would be as she recalled him in life – courteous and mannered.

Then she left, consumed with grief and guilt. Both her love and her lover had died in one explosive moment.

Of all the cases in this book, this is probably the one where the police are most certain about the identity of the person who caused the death of the victim. The prime suspect has been interviewed several times.

The police have never had enough evidence to make an arrest.

On 27 March 1994, Detective Senior Sergeant Hugh MacRae was quoted as saying that whoever dealt the fatal blow probably did not mean to kill Triggs.

"There doesn't appear to have been any attempt to mortally injure. There doesn't appear to have been premeditated violence. It appears to have been emotional and spontaneous. We're not looking at this as a brutal bashing intended to disfigure. This incident is quite obviously a tragedy which has arisen in the lives of two people... I feel for the offender because they know what they did and are going through all the uncertainty and the anxiety, and will pay the price emotionally."

A few days later, MacRae added: "It would be rather unlikely that a murder charge would come out of this homicide inquiry, but rather a charge of manslaughter. I believe she is a sensitive person who may suffer long-term consequences and loss of peace of mind about this. I wish she would come forward and we could lay this to rest. The guilt may well be worse than facing the charge of manslaughter."

To this date she has not yet come forward.

Unsc

15. Betty Marusich

The Vagrant of
Auckland Domain

The Auckland Domain is a swathe of green in the middle of Auckland's largest city, just as Central Park forms the heart of the concrete jungle of Manhattan in New York. There the comparison ends. After dark, Central Park becomes the domain of the mugger and murderer, while Auckland Domain is tame by comparison.

After dark, the Domain is the haunt of the odd vagrant and courting couple. By day, it is Auckland's playground. During the week, business executives jog through it or take their lunch. On Saturday mornings, it hosts the mud and thunder of rugby matches and on Sundays families walk their dogs and fly their kites.

That idyll was broken at 8.20 pm on 6 October 1995 when a jogger running along a track at the Parnell end of the Domain stumbled across a body.

It was hidden in dense bush, 50m off the track, resting against shrubs which had prevented it from rolling down a steep six-metre bank onto the railway lines. The partly decomposed body was lying face down in a semi-foetal position.

It was dressed in a large-size woman's Pickaberry sweatshirt that had a round neck and padded shoulders with a blue, black and red right sleeve and a mix of khaki and red on the front. Underneath was a purple knitted cardigan with a green triangular pattern. The body, which appeared to be that of a woman, wore no skirt and was naked below the waist.

Nearby was a yellow and green size 10 Nevica ski jacket, which was dirty, covered with mould and had blood on it. It had the word Recco on the front. Police hoped that identifying the jacket might lead them to the identity of the woman. The jacket had actually first been noticed about five days before by a man walking through the bush, but he had not noticed the body nearby.

The body was believed to be that of a European. There was a distinctive watch on her left wrist. It was large and black with a 4cm diameter white face with black Roman numerals. It was still ticking.

At first, the police were unsure of the identity of the victim. The body was too badly decomposed to offer any positive identification, or its age, or how long it had been there. The style of clothes at first led them to believe it might be a backpacker.

The area was cordoned off and a team of forensic scientists, including two pathologists who were visiting from Australia, made a thorough inspection of the scene. Then the body was removed in a body bag along with other items. A guard was mounted over the site and police began house-to-house inquiries.

After analysis of the body, the pathologist estimated that the dead woman had been between 168 and 170cm tall, had shoulder length fair hair and was probably aged between 50 and 65 years.

Several of her teeth were missing or broken. Her top jaw had four teeth in the front, one of them broken in half. Her bottom jaw had seven teeth. However, the police did not believe that the state of her teeth was due to any attack she might have suffered.

This led them to believe she might be one of two female vagrants who frequented the park. The large black watch she wore on her wrist was still set to pre-daylight saving time, which allowed police to calculate that the body must have lain undiscovered for a period of between nine and 21 days.

On 10 October, four days after the body was discovered, a local dentist came forward and identified the victim as 69-year-old vagrant Elizabeth "Betty" Marusich. A few years earlier, he had taken pity on her and given her free dental treatment.

For many years, eccentric Betty Marusich had been a familiar face in Auckland Domain. She had been born in New Zealand to Yugoslav parents. After leaving school, for a while she had worked at a Queen St florist shop. She later married and had one daughter. Her husband died in 1982 and shortly afterwards Betty became estranged from her daughter for reasons that are unknown. Either prior to this point or soon after, she went into a decline, starting to withdraw into her own world and she spent many years going in and out of mental hospitals. Her memory was very poor and she became withdrawn, not communicating with others.

She sold the Parnell house that she had shared with her husband and gradually lost the proceeds from the sale in subsequent property transactions. She stayed in hotels for two years until all her money ran out. Then she took to the streets, living in the St Heliers area for about three years before returning to Parnell, but this time not to a house, but her own patch at the Parnell end of the Domain, which she carved out of the bush.

She lived there in summer and winter with little protection from the wind and the rain.

During the day, she would wander around the area. Her daily schedule was to walk to Cafe Natatorium at the Olympic Pools at Newmarket. There she would take her standard breakfast of tea along with toast and marmalade. Once a week, she would enjoy a cooked breakfast there.

It was probably in the Cafe Natatorium with the echoing sounds of the swimming pool in the background that she felt the most comfortable. Though reclusive, she struck up probably her most binding relationship with the manager of the cafe, Debbie Meek, who took the time to chat to this obviously once-dignified woman who had fallen on hard times.

The rest of the day was spent walking around Parnell and Newmarket. On occasions, she was also seen as far away as Mission Bay. She would call in at the second-hand shops along the way and this was where she invested the meagre funds from her pension into old clothing in much the same way that a billionaire might invest his wealth in old masters.

Betty liked to buy bright clothes that she wore in unusual combinations. After her death, at various places around the Domain, the police discovered her neatly folded bundles of clothes that had been wrapped in plastic to protect them against the elements. She had probably forgotten about them long ago.

She would talk to the shopkeepers or the staff in the cafes where she ate, but only briefly, in her withdrawn manner. Those whose paths she crossed later recalled with some affection her benign presence. She was just a little old lady, who could have been anybody's grandmother, harmless and unassuming.

She still maintained something of her upbringing in her appearance, despite her lifestyle. She kept herself well groomed, always looking clean and sometimes wearing make-up. In earlier years, she had often paid for a hotel room – not to sleep there, but to take a shower. Sometimes she would be seen walking along mumbling to herself, but she never begged.

At the end of the day, she would head back towards her "home" in the Domain. As she did so, her world began to close around her again. Perhaps she began to become aware of the life she now lived compared to the life she had lived before. She undoubtedly would have preferred to be going home to a comfortable house with a fire in the hearth to warm her in the winter months.

But she would seem happy enough sitting in her deckchair in her "home" in the middle of the scrub. Sometimes, she could be seen keeping it clean and tidy, much like any housewife, and people who regularly used the park would often wave to her.

But as pleasant as the park is to walk or jog through, it has its dangers. Only a few months before her murder, Betty had witnessed an assault. The police had questioned her about this.

The post mortem showed that she had been dead for about two weeks. She was still alive on 18 September, which was the last time she had taken money out of her bank account.

It was calculated that she had disappeared somewhere between 18 and 21 September. The exact date is unknown because she had no contacts and no one missed her, so no missing person report was filed. During that time, someone had attacked her from behind, striking her on the head with a blunt instrument, at least once, but probably several times.

Even as her body lay in the mortuary, it seemed her spirit lived on because there were two sightings of her in Remuera, but these were of two women who looked like Betty.

The police were eager to locate her handbag, which she had been invariably seen with when alive but which was missing from the scene. The handbag, which was like a satchel, was made of vinyl or leather and had a soft texture like crocodile skin. It had two handles, two zips at the top and no shoulder strap. Inside were believed to be Betty's personal possessions, including hats and deodorant.

Also missing was a silver oval or heart-shaped locket that she had been wearing at the time. It was inscribed with the words, "To Mary 1972."

The hunt for her murderer was appropriately given the name of "Operation Wanderer" and the inquiry was headed by Detective Inspector Phil Jones. More than 80 officers worked up to six days a week and interviewed over 1500 people. Anybody who was a regular user of the Domain was interviewed. Joggers had to take a breather from their runs to answer questions, while records at Auckland Council were checked to see which council workers had worked there recently. The hunt went nationwide to investigate people who had committed similar crimes. Gradually each was eliminated from the inquiry.

The main problem the police came up against in their quest for her murderer was Betty's lifestyle. When a crime is committed, clues are deposited like sediment along the way. Files, letters, fingerprints, broken windows and anything else unusual provides pieces that build a picture which hopefully will ultimately form a clear image. An investigation resembles the slowly developing picture of a photographic negative.

Not only did Betty have no connections and no house, but also her body lay undiscovered and rained on by the elements for a full week before it was discovered. Whatever clues there were at the scene of her death were washed away. Some that remained were probably cleaned up by well-intentioned passersby. Incriminating evidence could well have been picked up and simply thrown in the rubbish bin.

One essential piece of evidence was Betty's "throne", her deck chair. It was an older-style, spring-loaded folding model with a faded cover of blue, white and pink fabric. It is possible that Betty was sitting in her deck chair when she was attacked. That deckchair was discovered by a passerby 40 metres from Betty's decomposing body.

Believing the metal framed chair had been abandoned, he took it home and cleaned it, intending to keep it for his own use. He later changed his mind and put it out in an inorganic rubbish collection in the Westmere area around mid to late December. Police appealed for anyone to come forward who might have picked it up out of the rubbish but the deckchair was never recovered.

Virtually every piece of junk that was lying in the Domain at the time was picked up by the police team and catalogued in the hope that they would provide a clue. One thing the police search did reveal was the large supply of women's underwear that had been abandoned in the Domain. Undergarments that were believed to belong to Betty were found 50 metres from her body.

A semen sample was also discovered and sent for analysis. The total number of exhibits collected ran to 2500.

On 22 December, a $20,000 reward was offered for information leading to the conviction of the killer, but nothing useful materialised from the offer and three months after the inquiry was started it was wound down and officers were reassigned to other cases.

Many people who had lost contact with Betty Marusich were touched by her death. It did not matter that she was an itinerant soul, dispossessed by society. She was a human being, and, belatedly, society decided to possess her again.

Old classmates from as far back as her primary school years paid for funeral notices to appear in the newspapers. At 2 pm on 5 November, about 150 people turned up for her non-religious memorial service in Auckland Domain, which was organised by the Parnell Community Centre.

The service was attended by many who had not even met

Betty but felt compassion for her. One who attended who did remember her well was Debbie Veasey, whose Parnell cafe Betty regularly visited.

The people who had gathered to commemorate Betty walked the track over which she had taken her last steps before listening to speeches and a poem. Then flowers were sprinkled over the clearing. The purpose of the service was also to reclaim the Domain as a public park and place of enjoyment rather than as the site of a brutal murder.

"We are a community. Betty was part of that community," said Mrs Cathy Romeyna, spokeswoman for the Community Centre.

When the inquiry was wound down, the list of suspects had been narrowed to eight men. Some of them had been avoiding the police and some had told inconsistent stories due to "memory lapses". None of them has been eliminated from the inquiry, but there was insufficient evidence to charge any of them with the murder.

One suspect was a 29-year-old Auckland man, who was remanded in custody until November 1995 to face four charges of sexual violation, aggravated robbery and wounding, separate incidents which had all occurred in the Domain.

The man in charge of the inquiry, Detective Inspector Phil Jones, who has since moved south to take over the police base in Queenstown, believes that the police have already talked to the murderer, who is on the list of the eight suspects.

Three years later, in December 1998, there was a sensational new development in the case when a builder repairing the roof of the St John the Baptist Catholic church in Parnell came across some old bags that were decaying on the roof.

The builder had needed an extension ladder to get onto the roof, so it seemed likely that someone had thrown them up there. The two bags, one leather and one canvas, were found to have belonged to Betty Marusich. The police seized further items in the vicinity of the church and these and the bags were sent for forensic testing.

Betty's death is the tragedy of somebody who chose to step outside the normal safeguards of society. She was attacked simply because she was vulnerable. She had little else to offer. The attacker might have believed she had money because she seemed able to afford to eat in cafes but that was paltry compared to what he would have got by burgling a house or robbing a bank.

It is possible that, despite Betty being an elderly woman, the motive was sexual gratification.

Though Betty had fallen on hard times she had never lost her basic goodness and honesty. On occasion when shopkeepers had given her something because she had no money, she had always gone back later to pay for it.

Those qualities were completely contrary to the person who made the cowardly attack on her. He crept up on a lonely old woman under cover of darkness. There were no locks to pick, no windows to force open. She had no walls to protect her and no telephone to call for help.

Though he may never be caught, he has already built a prison around himself by a cowardly assault on a harmless old woman.

16. Tania Furlan

Who Kidnapped
Baby Tiffany?

On Friday 26 July 1996, Victor Furlan left his Howick home at 6.15 am to go to work at Big Fresh supermarket as usual. He left behind his mother-in-law, his three children and his wife, Tania. He was never to see Tania alive again.

His mother-in-law, Shirley Bischelberger, had come over from Canberra to help look after the couple's two older children. Their third child, Tiffany, had been born prematurely in the National Women's Hospital in Auckland six weeks before. Tiffany was still being held in the special care birthing unit and Tania had to go into hospital four times a day to feed her.

Finally, on 25 July, Tiffany came home from hospital and Bischelberger was able to return to Canberra. While her plane was in mid-air, shocking events were taking place in Auckland. She did not find out about them until the plane landed in Canberra. By that time, the details had been phoned through to her husband, Kevin, who met her at the airport.

She came off the plane ready to tell him the news about their grandchildren in New Zealand, but instead she saw tears running down his face.

At 4.29 pm, Tania had phoned Victor at Big Fresh. He was not able to return her call until 4.50 pm. When he did, there was no answer. He tried again a minute later and again had no luck. When he tried to get through again four minutes later there was still no answer. He started to get concerned. When he phoned again at 5.12, someone finally picked up the phone. But it wasn't his wife. Instead it was his five-year-old daughter, Katrina.

He asked to speak to Tania and the child went looking for her mother. She returned to the phone shortly afterwards to tell her father, "Mum's hurt and bleeding."

Victor Furlan immediately called the police. He grabbed his cell phone and drove home, phoning again as he drove. Again it was Katrina who answered. He hung up to call an ambulance to the property, then phoned home again. The girls had gone nextdoor to the neighbour's house and this time it was the shocked neighbour who answered the phone.

The paramedics arrived to find Tania Furlan still alive, lying face down on the floor in a pool of blood.

Little Katrina just sat quietly on a sofa while they attended to her mother. She told the neighbour she had been playing in another room and did not see what had happened to her mother. Sonya, aged three, had also been playing in another part of the house.

Victor arrived home distraught about his wife but relieved that his two eldest daughters were safe, but then he realised – where was baby Tiffany?

It looked as if in addition to the brutal assault on Tania Furlan, the police also had a kidnapping to deal with.

At that moment, the six-week-old child was travelling in a car westwards. The killer or his or her accomplice had picked her up from her cot and placed her in a papoose-style baby carrier that was in the house, then carried her out of the house and put her in a vehicle.

At 6.20 pm, a Grafton resident, Faye Langdon, was parking her car in the Royal Oak Baptist Church car park, 18km away from Howick. Her thoughts about the game of squash she was about to play at the courts next door were interrupted by the sound of a baby crying.

She followed the sounds of the cries and found baby Tiffany wrapped in her cocoon-type sleeping bag sheltered under the eaves of the church from the light rain that was falling. The woman alerted the police and Tiffany was collected and taken to Starship children's hospital for observation. Whoever had left the child there had not only left her somewhere where she would be quickly found, but also well protected.

The police concluded that Tiffany had been dropped at the church between 5.45 and 6 pm. A red hatchback was seen driving out of the empty church car park at 5.55 pm. It turned left into Symonds St and drove on towards the Royal Oak roundabout. There was only one person in the car but the witness was unable to see if the driver was male or female.

Though the baby had been found, an abduction charge could still be levelled against the perpetrator of the crime, but there was now a far more serious charge to face, that of murder, because Tania Furlan had died of her injuries on the way to hospital.

Tania Furlan had been born in Australia Tania Maree Bischelberger. Her father was an Austrian immigrant,

Wilhelm Bischelberger. Her mother, Shirley, was Australian.

Tania and her younger brother Jason grew up in the suburb of Holder in Southern Canberra. She was a happy child with a particular fondness for cats. When she was older, she also enjoyed ballroom dancing. She met her future husband, Victor, aged 15, while she was at school.

He was the trainee manager at the local Woolworths store when she went to get some part-time work there. They fell in love and eventually married. In 1988, they moved into a new home in Isabella Plains, one of South Canberra's expanding upmarket suburbs.

There they blended in as a normal, happy family until Victor Furlan was made the manager of the Woolworth's Supermarket in Cooma, a tourist town at the foot of the Snowy Mountains.

Franklin's Big Fresh is part of the Woolworth's chain and in 1994 Victor Furlan was offered the position of manager of the Big Fresh store in Glenfield, on Auckland's North Shore.

The couple moved to New Zealand, settling in as just another suburban family enjoying the easygoing New Zealand lifestyle. Then on 26 July 1996, after seeing her mother off at the airport, Tania had taken Tiffany to the Howick Plunket Clinic to be weighed. Then she drove home. Her mother was still waiting for her flight at the airport and the two spoke by telephone.

At about 3 pm, Tania drove to Owairoa Primary School to pick up five-year-old Katrina and the two girls of a neighbour. At about 3.30 pm, she dropped off the neighbour's girls in Valnera Close, just around the corner from Brampton Rise. There she had a cup of coffee and chatted before driving home.

The next thing that is certain is that she called her husband at Big Fresh at 4.29 pm. No one knows why she made that call. It could have been just another ordinary call from a wife to a husband to tell him some news about the children or to ask him to bring some provisions home. Or it could have been that tragic events were already starting to unfold at the house on Brampton Rise.

Detective Inspector John Manning was placed in charge of the inquiry, leading a 30-strong investigation team. Manning was well known as the man who had led the team that captured Joseph Thompson, the South Auckland serial rapist.

House-to-house inquiries were carried out in the upmarket Cumbria Downs subdivision. The police took the fingerprints of anyone who might have visited the Furlan house.

At first, the police investigation centred on the theory that the crimes had been committed by a mentally deranged woman. It was suggested the woman might have lost her own baby recently and was trying to replace it by stealing someone else's. It was thought that perhaps the woman had some link to Tania Furlan and had targeted Tiffany.

At the autopsy, six two-centimetre indentations were discovered in Tania's skull. They were believed to have been caused by a hammer, possibly an engineer's hammer.

It was thought that the deranged woman might have knocked on the door of Tania's house in Brampton Rise. Perhaps Tania had recognised her from the hospital or somewhere else and had invited her inside, in a friendly manner. But when Tania had turned back towards the house, the woman had struck her six times on the back of the head with the hammer.

As there had been no hammer in the house before the incident, it was assumed the murderer must have brought the murder weapon with her.

The fact that she had selected the unusual papoose baby carrier to take the baby away seemed to prove the theory that she was a woman. Would any man have recognised it for what it was?

The police obtained court orders to view confidential records of patients who had been admitted to South

Auckland Health Services recently who had been suffering from a psychotic illness and who had also suffered a miscarriage, stillbirth or fertility problems.

Records from National Women's Hospital were examined. It was suspected that Tania Furlan's killer might have been on the ward at the same time. Inquiries were also made at Barnardos where Tania Furlan had babysat for working Howick couples by taking children into her own home. The search was also extended to Highland Park Kindergarten which Sonya attended, Owairoa Primary School which Katrina attended, and the Howick Plunket Clinic which Tania regularly attended.

Baby-snatching is a rare crime in New Zealand. In 1993, six-day-old James Collins was snatched from his cot at National Women's Hospital. The next day, the baby was found in Avondale. He had been abducted by a 24-year-old woman, Lisa Lula, who had had a baby at the age of 17 but had not been allowed any contact with him. She was sentenced to nine months' imprisonment for the abduction.

However, as far as the abduction of Tiffany was concerned, leading criminologist Professor Paul Wilson, former director of research at the Australian Institute of Criminology, warned that police should be suspicious of the baby-snatching theory. If it was a baby snatcher, he asked, "Why did the killer not keep the child?"

"Why did the abductor not take any of the child's belongings in the house to pacify her and why carry out the abduction at a time when all the other children were home and the husband would likely be due home from work on a Friday afternoon?"

He also felt that the striking of six hard blows to the back of the head was the way a man would kill rather than a woman. His belief was that the abduction was planned to obscure the real motive of the killing.

Another theory was that Tania had been killed by somebody with a grudge against her. Police made inquiries of a couple who had once been friendly with the Furlans but had recently fallen out with them. This couple's car and home were searched and their two children interviewed.

Twelve days after her murder, Tania's body was buried in Canberra at St Christopher's Cathedral in the suburb of Forrest. Almost 1000 people crammed into the cathedral, the same place where as a shy 19-year-old she had married Victor Furlan. He was there holding their two eldest daughters while eight-week-old Tiffany slept in a pink carry-cot.

A simultaneous memorial service was held at Our Lady Star of the Sea Catholic Church in Picton St, Howick. The service was attended by about 150 people, including Detective Inspector Manning and his second-in-command, Detective Sergeant Stu Mangnall.

Early in the inquiry, Victor Furlan had been ruled out of suspicion and he soon returned to Australia permanently with his three young daughters so that he could be close to family who would assist in raising his motherless children.

In New Zealand, police continued the investigation and on 1 November an arrest was made.

By this time, the inquiry had changed direction and it was a man who was charged with the murder of Tania Furlan. The accused was granted interim name suppression because the case had such a high profile and the attendant publicity might prejudice the eventual trial. The man was described only as an unemployed 32-year-old, who had been apparently about to leave the country on a false passport.

The accused was arrested in Dunedin and flown to Auckland where he appeared in the Otahuhu District Court. It was crown prosecutor Simon Moore who requested that the media be banned from showing footage of the accused entering and leaving court, even with a blanket over his head. This was upheld by the judge who banned anything being written about him which could identify him including details of his hair colour, clothing, height and race. An artist's sketch of him in the courtroom was confiscated. The identity of the accused remained a mystery to the public.

The accused did not enter a plea, but said he was innocent and wanted a hearing at the earliest opportunity.

On 13 December, the name suppression was lifted by Judge David Harvey in the Otahuhu District Court after a 90-minute debate by counsel. The accused's counsel, Paddy Driscoll, then indicated that he would lodge an appeal in the High Court. The judge was then forced to issue an order reinstating name suppression until the appeal could be heard.

The appeal was heard on 19 December 1996, and the Appeal Court judges saw no reason why the man charged with the murder of Tania Furlan should remain anonymous any longer. He was named as Christopher John Lewis, the same man who had a record as an escaper and bank robber, one of the most notorious criminals in New Zealand's history, especially for his attempt in 1981, as a teenager, to fire a bullet at the Queen.

Some said Lewis was a psychopath, some said he was still a wayward youth. Many of his activities were bizarre in the extreme, but what about murder and abduction? Were they his style?

At the depositions hearing at the Otahuhu District Court on 24 February, the Crown put forward the case that Lewis had murdered Tania Furlan in a botched kidnap attempt. The police theory was that Lewis knew that Victor Furlan was the manager at Glenfield Big Fresh and would have access to the safe. His plan was to kidnap Tania Furlan or her baby and use her as leverage to get his hands on the cash takings from the safe.

According to a criminal associate of Lewis who was prepared to give evidence against him, what happened in the missing 43 minutes of phone calls between Tania and her husband was that Lewis had gone to the house disguised as a deliveryman. Inside the box he was supposed to be delivering was a hammer.

He knocked on the door and it was answered by Tania. Then Lewis asked her for a pen to sign for the delivery.

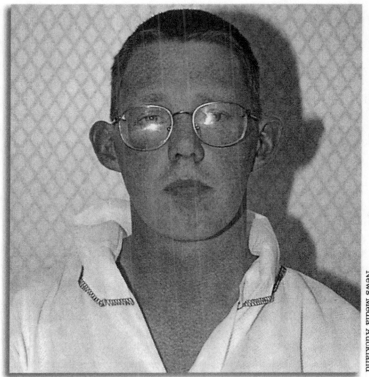

The grim face of a habitual criminal — Christopher John Lewis charged with the murder of Tania Furlan.

News Media Auckland

When she turned to get one, Lewis followed her into the house, taking the hammer out of the box. He attacked her from behind, hitting her on the head with it.

He had only intended one stunning blow, but when she fell like a stone to the ground he realised what he had done and, in a frenzy of blows, finished her off.

Then he left a ransom note and took the baby, depositing her at Royal Oak Church. Confused about what he had done, perhaps realising the enormity of it, he then returned to the house to retrieve the ransom note.

Footprints at the scene of the crime matched the soles of Reebok running shoes found at Lewis' home. Lewis had won the Reeboks in a competition from a shoe shop. He said they were so comfortable that he had worn them all the time, causing them to smell. This had been exacerbated by a kitten urinating on them at one point. As a result of this, Lewis got into the habit of leaving them outside the door at night.

He said that just after his girlfriend's birthday, on 15 July 1996, the shoes mysteriously disappeared. Just as mysteriously, two weeks later they reappeared.

Evidence was given concerning the indentations found on the notepad at Lewis' Helensville sleepout. Gordon Sharfe, a forensic document examiner, said that the top pages had been ripped out of a pad which had been found there, leaving marks on the pages below.

Two main techniques were used to highlight them. One was a simple test that any child could perform, shining oblique lighting across the page to highlight the indentations.

A more specialised technique employed electrostatic detection equipment. Here an electrical charge was applied to the plastic film covering the documents to reveal any indentations. Then an oppositely charged black toner was used to show up the image.

Sharfe testified that he found two different styles on the notepad. One was in Lewis' hand. The other was in a different hand, which he said was disguised writing by Lewis. Messages in the disguised hand included such phrases as "If you follow, you never see wife", "Come alone" and "When get money you will get wife 36 hours later."

However, Sharfe testified under cross-examination that he could not identify the author of the disguised writings. They could have been by Lewis' hand or anyone else.

Andrew Collett, who was a member of Lewis' martial arts

school, gave evidence that Lewis had suggested to him a scheme where they kidnapped a child. They would then send a ransom note to the child's wealthy grandfather, and after they got the cash, they would kill the child to avoid being identified. When Collett expressed his revulsion at this, Lewis apparently told him, "It didn't matter... it was just a soul."

More of Lewis' strange schemes were aired in court. These included going to Queenstown, killing all the local police and ransacking the town before escaping in a microlite aircraft. Another was to steal a boat so they could rob a bank on Waiheke Island.

Did Lewis really intend to carry out these bizarre plans or were they just idle fantasy, especially as Collett admitted they had been concocted by Lewis when he was under the influence of cannabis?

Another mad scheme was related by another witness. This involved kidnapping a woman, holding her to ransom and demanding $30,000 from her father. The money was supposed to be dropped in a rubbish bin at the West Auckland beach of Piha. An accomplice would then pick it up and paddle around to another bay on a surfboard where Lewis would be waiting.

Another plan Lewis had put forward, probably the strangest of the lot, was to track down and assassinate those responsible for the Rainbow Warrior bombing.

Lewis' former girlfriend, whose name was suppressed, testified that Lewis wanted to buy some land to build a martial arts facility and was always coming up with wild and fanciful schemes to raise the cash. In 1995, he had signed a lease on a warehouse in Glenfield which had been his dojo, but he was always struggling financially. This, the Crown contended, was the motive for his attempted extortion.

The police had evidence that Lewis shopped at Glenfield Big Fresh. One witness was prepared to state that he had seen a poster advertising Lewis' Ninja training school on the Glenfield Big Fresh noticeboard.

The name of the Crown's final witness was also suppressed. He told the court that he had met Lewis in a holding cell and that Lewis had told him that he was accused of murder. When the man asked him if he did it, Lewis replied "yes" in a stern voice as if he was saying "exactly what he meant".

At the end of the six-day depositions hearing, the judge, David Harvey, found that there was a prima facie case to answer. Lewis was remanded in custody until 9 April when a High Court date was set for November.

Lewis never made it to trial. Late in 1997, he decided that his life had reached a dead end and there was nowhere further for him to go. If found guilty of the crime, he would certainly be sentenced to life imprisonment. If acquitted, the charge would still taint him for the rest of his life.

No one can know for sure what Lewis was thinking in his last moments. He practised martial arts and claimed to be a ninja master. He seemed to have some understanding and appreciation of eastern philosophy, including making the distinction that people were souls who inhabited bodies.

His final act in life might have been a quite deliberate attempt to separate his spirit from the problems that it was beset by. To take him out of the impossible situation he had found himself in so that he could start anew.

Or it could have been an act of utter despair.

His last action certainly carried his mark, because it was unusual and creative. Cells are built to stop prisoners committing suicide, but Lewis tore away a power point, touched the live wires and continued to make contact with them, the electricity coursing through his body until he was dead.

So the question was never answered in a court of law whether or not Christopher Lewis murdered Tania Furlan and abducted her baby Tiffany.

Lewis claimed to have an alibi for the time when Tania was killed. He said he was taking his girlfriend to a yoga class. Though she had been granted name suppression by the court, she later chose to go on TV3 and publicly proclaim his innocence and support his alibi.

Police quickly moved to refute this by releasing the documentation of a police interview with her in which she had said, "I do not know where I was during Friday 26 July 1996. I possibly picked up my son somewhere around 4 pm, but I'm not sure.

"He may have gone to the dojo. I don't know where he was that afternoon. I don't keep a diary."

She also had a conviction for lying on Lewis' behalf. Shortly after the Furlan murder, she made a false declaration on a passport application by Lewis. The police said that the passport application had been made so that Lewis could flee the country.

In his autobiography, "Last Words", which was posthumously published in 1997, Lewis claimed that he had applied for the passport under a false name simply because he did not believe that any country would give him a visa with his criminal record. At the time, he said, he and his girlfriend were planning to sail a yacht to Chile.

He knew someone who did not have or need a passport so he paid that man to apply for a passport in the name of Chris Lewis. After the first application was put in, Lewis wanted to speed up the process and so he put in a second express application. By this time, the man had got cold feet and phoned up the passport office to cancel both applications.

At this point, the authorities smelt a rat and investigated.

In October 1996, Lewis' girlfriend pleaded guilty in the Christchurch District Court to making a false attestation on a passport form and was fined $350 plus costs.

Lewis was arrested in the garden of his mother's house where he was camping with his girlfriend. The media insisted he had been hiding out there. Lewis said that he was merely on holiday.

An apparently incriminating piece of evidence was that a toy gun was found hidden under the bonnet of Lewis' car. Though a toy, it was a good imitation and most people would have believed it was the real thing. Lewis claimed he had hidden it there because he did not want his girlfriend's young son to be frightened by it.

In his autobiography, Lewis sings the familiar lament of the criminal that at the time of the incident he had gone straight. But even in this book he still admits to growing marijuana plants which he was hoping to make a profit from of about $6000. It also seems he was responsible for two aggravated robberies after 26 July.

During one of them, the robber was caught on video camera. Though he wore a hood pulled over his head, the face looks unmistakably like Chris Lewis.

In a letter to his girlfriend before his death, which was basically his suicide note, Lewis professed his innocence in the murder of Tania Furlan. This theme is continued through his autobiography.

So was Lewis the killer?

It was an unusual crime for him to commit, though many of his crimes were unusual. He could have done it, but did he do it?

One of the lingering enigmas about Christopher John Lewis was that it was uncertain exactly what his potential for violence was. He was supposed to have tried to assassinate the Queen and yet the bullet flew harmlessly elsewhere.

That same year, when a teenage Lewis robbed a bank, his gun went off and though the bullet thudded harmlessly into the counter it could have just as easily killed someone. Lewis claimed this was an accident.

Another time, when Lewis was holed up in the Port Hills above Christchurch, he apparently hatched a plan which he noted in his diary to go down into Christchurch and murder a family. He did go down, entered a house and walked around it as the family slept, but in the end all he did was steal a wallet.

So was Lewis a psychopath as some claim, or more of a Walter Mitty character who operated on the wrong side of the law? In his autobiography he comes across as a multi-faceted personality. He is intelligent and aware, but prone to childish naivety, all of this probably best captured when he gave himself some vocational counselling one night during a walk along the beach.

His thinking went like this: with his prison record, he was unlikely to get a job. He disliked theft and burglary because he did not like taking people's personal possessions. Bank robbery was different. He was only stealing from faceless institutions and the money was replaced anyway by insurance companies. He came to the inevitable conclusion that bank robbery was the only vocation for which he was truly suited.

Some of his solutions to problems were bizarre in the extreme, such as the time he tried to escape from Dunedin to Christchurch by sea kayak. He only lasted a short time in the water before being forced to turn back. It would probably have taken him several days to kayak through open seas to Christchurch. The plan had been courageous but entirely unrealistic.

Before the Furlan case, it appears he did make genuine attempts to earn a living, though none of these seemed to last very long. Nor was his dojo a howling success.

So did Lewis hatch the fantastic plan to kidnap the wife and baby of a supermarket manager, hoping to gain access to the safe or that the cash-rich supermarket chain would be willing to pay a huge ransom for the baby's return?

It was the sort of crazy plan he might have come up with, but would he have enacted it? If so, how would he have gone about it? It was unusual for the so-called Ninja expert to smash a helpless housewife on the head with a hammer. Perhaps he believed that he had such control of the hammer that with a single strike he would use just the right amount of force to give her a stunning blow. When he realised he had used too much force, did he snap and finish off his victim with a flurry of blows?

Then did he snatch the baby either to divert attention from the murder or to continue his kidnapping plan? Did he then return to pick up his ransom note before the body was discovered and then abandon the baby beside a church in Royal Oak? If so, why didn't he just return the baby home?

Between the times that Victor Furlan was last phoned by his wife and the time that her body was discovered, 43 minutes elapsed. That was sufficient time for Lewis to have dropped off the baby at the church and return to pick up the ransom note. He may also have had an accomplice.

If Lewis had gone to trial, would the evidence against him have been strong enough to ensure a conviction? In the end, it might have rested on his smelly old Reeboks. If the prosecution had been able to prove that his was the shoe that had made the impression at Tania Furlan's house, then he would probably have been convicted.

If the defence had been able to prove that he owned a shoe that hundreds of others in New Zealand might have owned, then he may well have been acquitted. The imprint of the training shoe was the only direct evidence that linked him to the crime.

There are many other questions that because of Lewis' suicide will remain unanswered.

NOTE

At the end of March 1999, as this book was at the printers, there was another twist on the Tania Furlan case when police revealed that the man who had fingered Lewis for the murder had himself been arrested on a separate murder charge. Lewis claimed in "Last Words" that this man, who went by the pseudonym "Jimmy the Weasel", was the real murderer and had borrowed his shoes to commit it.

A new police review of the case now seems certain.

17. Kayo Matsuzawa

The Body in
the Cupboard

Tuesday 22 September 1998 seemed like just another day for Dennis Groves as he made his way along Queen St to the Centrecourt Building where he was carrying out routine maintenance, doing the monthly alarm check for his employer Wormald. He entered the building and climbed the steps of the stairwell off which was the fire alarm panel cupboard. It was locked as usual.

He took the key out of his pocket and unlocked it. When he opened the door, he noticed that somebody had been using the cupboard for storage. Inside the cupboard they had placed one of those mannequins you see in the front windows of fashion shops. This mannequin was small, thin and unclothed, standing rigidly in the stance in which no doubt it had been cast.

But as he stared at it, even though he could see no marks or injuries or blood, he knew suddenly that this was not a life-sized doll, but the shell of what had once been a living person, frozen in death by rigor mortis.

The body was that of a Japanese woman who was about 1.48m tall with straight, dark hair. The body weighed about 50kg and examination showed that it had received extensive dental work. Forensic experts estimated the decaying body had been in the cupboard for about a week.

The body was soon confirmed to be that of 29-year-old Kayo Matsuzawa, an overseas visitor from Japan. Kayo was from Yamagata in northern Japan.

It was the second such tragedy the small town of Yamagata had suffered in recent times. Another resident of the town, 22-year-old Afichiko Okuyama, was murdered in Cairns in September 1997 in similar circumstances. A week after she disappeared, her naked and decaying body was discovered in a local swamp. She had been lured into a warehouse and beaten to death. A 16-year-old youth was convicted of her murder only a few days after her compatriot Kayo Matsuzawa disappeared in Auckland.

Kayo had been working as an office worker at a seafood distribution company when she decided to come to New Zealand out of a sense of adventure and a desire to improve her English.

She was friendly, if shy, with a tendency to hide her nervousness with a smile. She enjoyed skiing and the movies, especially "Titanic", which she had seen four times. When she had taken a trip to Dunedin, she had asked someone to take her photograph on the bow of a boat with her arms spread out wide imitating the movie's heroine.

She arrived in Christchurch about a year before she disappeared. At first she lived at a home-stay while she studied at an English language school in the city. She later moved to a flat, which she shared with another Japanese woman. Using Christchurch as a base, she had toured around other parts of the South Island.

She had worked in the Thai Tasty restaurant in Gloucester St in Christchurch where she was popular with the other staff. Just before she left, one of them took a photograph of her in the restaurant. It was to be the last recorded image of a very much alive Kayo Matsuzawa.

On 11 September, she flew from Christchurch for a two-week holiday in Auckland. She was planning to come back to Christchurch when she had done all her sightseeing, then to go on to Australia in November where she was scheduled to attend her cousin's wedding at which she would be her family's representative in Australia.

On her arrival in Auckland, she booked into a Queen St backpackers hostel, where she paid in advance for a short stay and left a deposit for her room key. She intended to stay in the centre of Auckland for only three days before heading north to do more sightseeing. Then she put her belongings in her room and went out. The hostel locked its doors at 11 pm. After that, only key holders could get into the building.

The next morning, her room was found to be tidy and clean. It was not clear if Kayo had neatly made her own bed or had not returned that night.

After her body was found, the police began the laborious task of searching through her belongings to try to work out what, if anything, could be missing. From that they were able to determine that her small black knapsack was gone.

It was of a type that could be obtained only in Japan with two back pockets, a cross-over back-strap and a band which clipped at the waist. Police believed that she had the bag in her possession when she was killed.

Also missing were her camera, a pair of black trousers, a pair of black shoes, a pair of white jeans, two pairs of Ritz socks, a white push-up bra, a bus pass and her Cashflow card. The police believed that the murderer, in his haste to dispose of this evidence, had pushed them into a roadside rubbish bin which would have been collected by the rubbish carts and transferred to the Greenmount landfill tip in East Tamaki.

The police would not reveal why they were so certain about this although it was known that police had searched through footage taken by eleven security cameras in central Auckland at about the time of Kayo's murder.

It was generally believed that the security cameras had caught someone suspiciously dumping items into a refuse bin in Queen St. Police concentrated their scene-of-crime inquiries onto an area within 40 square metres of the Centrecourt Building while a seven-man investigation team moved to the Greenmount tip in East Tamaki. After discussions with the dump manager, the detectives concentrated on two specific areas at depths of 500mm and 1500mm.

The police were highly hopeful of finding something there and it was significant that the officer leading the search through the stinking rubbish was the man in charge of the inquiry, Detective Senior Sergeant Kevin Baker. But after four days of sifting through the accumulated refuse, the police announced they had only found items of minor significance. But were they items that had belonged to Kayo?

With the help of interpreters, the police interviewed students at the English language school which was situated in the Centrecourt Building where Kayo's body was found.

Kayo had come to Auckland alone. She did not know anyone in the city and had not arranged to meet anyone. The building where she was found was located 200 metres from the Queen St backpackers hostel where she had checked in. It was likely that she had gone to the English language school intending to make contact with other Japanese travellers.

She was sighted in Parnell on the afternoon of Friday 11 September with two men, believed to be Japanese. The witness said that Kayo had asked her for directions back to the central city, which she had written down in the back of her diary.

The following day on 12 September she was seen at the backpackers' hostel in the company of two men and a woman. That was the last sighting of her. After that, she faded into the background, just another tourist in a city of tourists.

On 30 September, Kayo's father, uncle, brother and cousin flew in from Japan. Two days later, on Friday 2 October, she was cremated at a private ceremony in Auckland. Also in attendance to pay their last respects were her cousin and fiancée, whose wedding she had planned to attend. The wedding was postponed.

Later they went to the fire alarm cupboard where her body had been discovered and held another ceremony, this time saying prayers and burning incense. A bunch of flowers was then placed outside the cupboard door.

The next day her family immediately flew back to Japan with her ashes. They had no reason to stay, nor could they bear to remain longer in the country which their relative had ventured to and in which she had died.

Ironically, as the police struggled to find clues for the murder, the woman who in death was at first believed to be a mannequin was represented by a mannequin which the police displayed in the downtown area of Auckland to raise public awareness of the case.

According to the Backpackers' Accommodation Council, about 150,000 backpackers throng New Zealand every year. Female Japanese backpackers often travel alone. Apparently it is seen as Western and hip. Kayo should have been safe in a crowded city so how was she killed and where? Was it in the building where she was found?

Probably, as the killer would have had great difficulty surreptitiously bringing her body down Queen St. But where did she meet the murderer? Was it at the English language school, at the hostel or somewhere else?

Wide eyed and innocent, Kayo was new to Auckland and knew no one there. When she arrived, it seems she immediately sought to make contact with her fellow Japanese. After she had stowed her belongings in her room, she went out in search of them. She knew she would undoubtedly find some of her countrymen at the local language school. Did she come all the way from Japan to New Zealand to be murdered by a Japanese person?

The likelihood is that she knew her murderer, if only briefly, and she trusted him enough to go to some lonely place with him. Whether he intended sex or murder at that point is unclear, but it is certain that he intended to take advantage of this pretty, shy girl with a fringe falling down over her eyes.

Did he lure her to the Centrecourt Building late at night? He would have known that he had the strength to overpower her. It is almost certain he sexually assaulted her or raped her. That was probably the reason why her body was naked when found. It is possible that he could have stripped her naked to hide any evidence that might have been on her clothes but a rapist needs to at least partially undress his victim to perform his foul act. He will almost never dress her again, so disrobing always tends to point to a sexual crime.

As she lay dead in his arms, he knew that he had committed the ultimate act both against his own conscience and against society. Human life is sacrosanct. The taking of it is the greatest theft, for it can never be given back. Perhaps the murderer was shocked at what he had done, looking down at this body that was little bigger than that of a child.

Perhaps he felt the urge to go and confess. And that is generally the thin line between the murderer and the manslaughterer. It has often been observed that when murder is intended, the murderer will attempt to cover up his crime, while the manslaughterer will often admit to the accidental killing.

Kayo's killer chose the route of the murderer. His senses were now keen to everything around him, the fall of approaching footsteps, the opening of a door, any distant sounds of life, for no one must know what he was doing or what he had done.

It was his secret now and his alone. There could never be another unguarded moment in his life. He must carry this secret with him wherever he went, as heavy a burden as the body he picked up and carried to the fire alarm cupboard.

It is not clear how he unlocked the fire alarm cupboard. That is the "key" to the whole mystery. Only about 10 people had access to the keys to the cupboard, but police inquiries did not produce evidence to link any of them with the crime. The building was also monitored by a card access system linked to a computer. Hundreds of people had access to the building, any one of whom could have been the murderer.

If the cupboard was locked, he should not have been able to get her into it. No matter how deranged the killer might have been to commit the ultimate crime, hiding her in the cupboard was the act of an intelligent and orderly mind.

The police believe that the killer also had forensic knowledge by the way he delayed the finding of the body and removed all the clothes and all other evidence. He left little if any DNA evidence. The pathologist was not even able to determine the cause of death because decomposition was too far advanced, but strangulation or some form of poisoning were the most likely causes.

In February 1999, the police posted a reward of $50,000 for information leading to the conviction of whoever had killed Kayo Matsuzawa. Whether that will help to flush out her murderer remains to be seen.

The Last Word

I began writing this book from the point of view of the investigative process of finding the murderer, but the more I wrote, the more I also found I was getting to know the victims.

For reasons they did not have full control over, their life came to an abrupt end. A shockingly abrupt end. Just before that moment, those people were still living with dreams and plans and hopes and unfinished commitments in their relationships with others. When we are fired from a job, we are given the opportunity to clear our desk, or when a marriage ends there is the carving-up of the possessions and time spent with children. Painful as that may be, at least we get the opportunity to do it.

But violent death when decided by another, is sudden and horrible. Far too sudden and far too horrible. If death was simply death there would be no problem, for all would end there anyway, but if life continues in some form after death, then it must be agonising for those victims not to have their final say.

For relatives of the victim, the pain is also in the suddenness with which the loved one is stolen from them and the inability to communicate with them. The grief at a funeral or memorial service, while no doubt springing out of that deep well of love, is also exacerbated by the deep frustration of not being able to communicate with the departed.

Part of my job as a writer is to help other people to tell their stories. I hope that in some small way, in the pages of this book, I have been able to complete the stories of those who suffered the slings and arrows of fate in the ultimate defeat.

It is society which seeks to find and punish the murderer, the person who has been murdered just wants to have their final say.

Bibliography

"The Bad, the Very Bad and the Ugly" – Tony Williams, Hodder Moa Beckett, 1998.

"Beyond Reasonable Doubt" – David Yallop, Penguin Books, 1978.

"By a Person or Persons Unknown" – George Joseph, the Law Book Company, 1982.

"Greed" – Richard Hill, Pan Books, 1991.

"Guilty on the Gallows" – Sherwood Young, Grantham House, 1998.

"Justice without Fear or Favour" – Kevin Ryan, Hodder Moa Beckett, 1997.

"Kirsa, a Mother's Story" – Robyn Jensen, David Ling, 1994.

"Last Words" – Christopher John Lewis, Howling at the Moon, 1997.

"Metro" magazine.

Newsmedia Library.

"NZ Herald".

"NZ Listener".

"North & South" magazine.

"Techniques of Crime Scene Investigation" – Arne Svensson and Otto Wendell, American Elsevier Publishing, 1971.

"Traces of Guilt" – Guy Brown and Peter Llewellyn, Collins, 1991.

"Will to Kill" – Fred McLean, IPL Books, 1998.

"Without Fear or Favour, 150 Years Policing Auckland" – Senior Sergeant Owen J. Cherrett, published by the New Zealand Police.

"Working Girls, Women in the New Zealand Sex Industry Talk to Jan Jordan" – Jan Jordan, Penguin Books, 1991.